Second edition

ABOUT THE AUTHORS

Following publication of the first edition of *An ABC of NLP*, Joseph Sinclair spent five years as Managing Director of a shipping line in the north of England, before reverting to full-time writing. A second edition of his earlier book on refrigerated transport is being published shortly. He has also co-written, with Michael Mallows, *Peace of Mind is a Piece of Cake,* the first in a series of books on self-help and empowerment.

Stephen Bray was born and lives in Dorset. Trained in the disciplines of Fritz Perls, Milton Erickson and Virginia Satir, the original models for Neuro-linguistic Programming, Stephen studied NLP with the NLP Training Program in London and the Dynamic Learning Centre for NLP, Santa Cruz, California. He is a psychotherapist, a trainer and an organisational consultant who has been living and practising NLP since 1986.

an ABC of NLP

Second edition

Joseph Sinclair
with additional material by Stephen Bray
Illustrations by ALB

ASPEN
London, England

First edition published in May 1992

ISBN 0 9513660 1 7

Text copyright © 1992 Joseph Sinclair
Illustrations copyright © 1992 Albert Saunders

New edition published in September 1998 by
Container Marketing Limited,
106 Holders Hill Road,
London NW4 1LL
England
under the ASPEN imprint

ISBN 0 9513660 3 3

Text copyright © 1998 Joseph Sinclair and Stephen Bray
Illustrations copyright © Container Marketing Limited

Printed by
Redwood Books
Kennet Way
Trowbridge
Wiltshire BA14 8RN
England

All rights reserved. No part of this book may be reproduced or transmitted in any form, electronic or mechanical, including photocopy, or any information storage and retrieval system, without permission in writing from the publisher.

CONTENTS

Introduction 6

Foreword by Stephen Bray 7

Table of Illustrations 8

An ABC of NLP 11

References 143

INTRODUCTION

An ABC of NLP was written and published in 1992 to fill a perceived need. It seemed to me that the language of NLP often resulted in a slippage between the medium and the message it sought to convey. *An ABC of NLP* was an attempt to bridge the chasm which resulted from that slippage. It was addressed predominantly to those beginners who were experiencing the same difficulties I had faced in their situation, and who needed a work of reference written in simple everyday language which would help their comprehension of the NLP books they were reading or courses they were taking.

The book has sold modestly well over the years and I have often been asked if it was my intention to write a sequel which would be addressed to the more advanced students. I resisted this appeal because I felt that it would run counter to the specific selling point of the *ABC*, namely its simplicity.

Eventually, however, the time came when few further copies of the book were available and a decision had to be taken about republishing.

At this point I mentioned my dilemma to Stephen Bray. Stephen seemed excited at the idea of revising the existing volume and updating some of its concepts, and his enthusiasm fired my own imagination with the possibility of a book which would continue to appeal to the beginner, but might also have something of merit for the Master Practitioner.

This book is the result of that collaboration. My main regret in reprinting the book is that my great friend and collaborator, Albert Saunders (ALB – the illustrator of the original edition) is no longer with us to share the excitement and joy of this new venture. Albert lived just long enough to see the *ABC of NLP* in print and then, alas, suffered a fatal heart attack following a course of chemotherapy.

It is with both sadness and joy at the continued inclusion of his charming illustrations that I dedicate this book to his memory.

JOSEPH SINCLAIR

FOREWORD BY STEPHEN BRAY

Contributing to the second edition of *An ABC of NLP* has been a challenging but rewarding undertaking. The challenge has arisen because Joe and I are different. He writes in a smooth rounded style which simplifies the content to the minimum necessary. In short his style is the embodiment of the elegance principle. The result is a surface structure which will be a delight to anyone approaching NLP for the first time.

Unfortunately, I live in a world populated by medical researchers and crusty academics. Such people do not thrive on surface structure but require depth in their understanding. The original *ABC of NLP* aimed to provide a readable explanation of NLP terms for those grappling with learning this craft. In this revised edition my contribution has been to attempt to underpin some of the NLP terms introduced in the first edition, with related concepts such as *System Theory*.

Joe envisaged that the *ABC of NLP* would, like any dictionary, usually be referred to when reading another text rather than read from cover to cover like a novel. this worried me, as I know a number of people who might be tempted to buy the dictionary and try to write their own novel, but lose the plot early in chapter one.

For this reason, in my contributions, I have attempted to clarify my model of NLP and suggest some ways in which I believe it valuable to apply NLP concepts. I am especially hopeful that it may help people to get thinking in original ways.

Some time ago I told Joe that I see NLP as more than a set of disunited techniques all marketed under the NLP brand. The techniques themselves may seem disparate but they are all linked within the person and, although there are boundaries between, for example, working with specific behaviours and working with a person's identity, working with one is likely to affect the other.

Joe responded by saying: "This is just your model of the world". He was right to do so.

TABLE OF ILLUSTRATIONS

AMBIGUITY	14
ANCHORING	16
CHUNKING	27
COMMUNICATION	30
CONFUSION	33
CONTEXT REFRAMING	36
DELETION	41
DISSOCIATION	44
DISTORTION	45
EYE ACCESSING CUES	51/52
FINGER POINTERS	55
FUTURE PACING	58
INCONGRUENCE	64
INTERNAL REPRESENTATIONS	66
LANGUAGE	69
LEARNING, FOUR STAGES OF	72
MEMORY	77

[A META MODEL CHART IS ON PAGE 81]

MISMATCHING	84
MODEL OF THE WORLD	90
NEGOTIATION	92
NOMINALIZATION	97
PACING	100
PARAMESSAGES	101
PATTERN-INTERRUPTS	103
PLACATOR	107
RAPPORT	111
REPRESENTATIONAL SYSTEMS	115
STEPPING	127
STRATEGY	128
SYNTACTIC AMBUIGITY	132
UNSPECIFIED NOUNS	140

A NOTE ON FORMAT

Text in ***bold italics*** will direct you to other, more detailed information on associated subjects.

ACCESSING CUES

Slight changes of behaviour that help to trigger and indicate which *representational* or *sensory system* a person is using to process information internally. They comprise involuntary eye movement patterns, breathing patterns, changes in posture or muscle tone, changes in vocal tone or tempo, facial tone coloration, gestures and body movements. Most of us favour one sensory system above the others: some of us tend habitually to think in pictures (visual), others think in sounds (auditory) and some think kinaesthetically (feelings). These ways of processing may be context based, for example architects may process information visually at work, but organise their family life kinaesthetically in terms of comfort. Studying the cues is a way of eliciting which sensory system is being favoured.

There are simple ways of eliciting specific sensory based responses by asking questions designed to induce auditory, visual, or kinaesthetic responses. For example: "What's your favourite piece of music?" or "Can you hear yourself reciting your favourite poem?" are auditory questions. A question such as "How would you look with green hair?" would require the person to imagine something which has never been experienced; this is known as a *visual construct* (V^c) question as against a *visual remembered* (V^r) question such as "Which colour is at the top of the traffic light?". Kinaesthetic accessing questions might include, "How does it feel to stroke velvet?" or "What would it feel like to walk on Mars?" Such kinaesthetic (*K*) questions may be predicated to access a memory or a construct; however the eye accessing cue will be directed to the same location for most people.

We are able, to an extent, to control or modify our neurological state by the way we breathe, alter our posture or muscle tone, use eye movements, modify our vocal tones or tempo, etc. Changing the tempo of our breathing, for example, enables us more easily to access in a kinaesthetic mode; tilting our head to one side is a way of accessing the auditory sensory system; glancing upwards and to the right helps us to construct visual images. The most powerful of all these behavioural patterns, as a determinant of state, is that of breathing.

Accessing Cues are sometimes called Entry Cues because people may, for example, visualise a portion of a memory before they hear it, or they may, for example; see something which leads them into hearing it.
[See *Auditory, Breathing Patterns, Eye Accessing Cues, Failure into Feedback Strategy, Four Tuple, Kinaesthetic, Miller George A, Neurology, Relational Operator, TOTE, Visual*]

A^c
A symbol representing Auditory Constructed: an internally generated sound which is not a remembered experience.
[See *TOTE notation*]

A^d
A symbol representing Auditory Digital: i.e. self talk.
[See *Part, Tape Loops, TOTE notation*]

ADVANCED MODELLING STRATEGY
The concept of modelling is central to the practice of NLP. The advanced modelling strategy is a unified approach to modelling developed by **Robert Dilts** and others. It enables an individual to learn to perform a task in the same way as adopted by an expert.
1. Identify a specific skill to be modelled and also a model(s).
2. Elicit at least three examples of the model performing the skill.
3. Calibrate the models for:
    a) **Accessing Cues**
    b) **Predicates, Meta/Milton Model Patterns**
    c) **Physiology**
    d) **Sensory Systems, Strategies & Sub Modalities**
    e) **Meta Programme Patterns**

    f) *Beliefs, Values, Conceptual Maps*
    g) *Logical Levels*
Determine the similarities in all of the examples.
4. Find a person or a situation who is either unable to perform the skill, or who is unable to perform the skill in a particular *context*.
5. Using the same *criteria* as in step 3 determine the critical differences in these *counter examples*.
6. Change all the critical factors in the counter examples to match those of the model until the skill can be repeated in the counter example.
7. Vary the critical factors until you have determined the minimum number of factors needed to perform the skill.
[See also: *Elegance Principle*]

A^e
A symbol representing Auditory External: hearing an externally generated sound, such as listening to music or hearing a tap dripping.
[See *TOTE notation*]

AFFERENT TRACK
[See *New Code NLP*]

A^i
A symbol representing Auditory Internal: an internally generated sound.
[See *TOTE notation*]

AMBIGUITY
The experience of encountering sentences which have more than one meaning. For example: *I must leave you to discover an example*, or *We agree with striking workers*. In the transformational model of language [See **Transformational Grammar**], a **Surface Structure** is said to be ambiguous if it can be derived from more than one **Deep Structure**.
    Eric Partridge[1] points out that ambiguity is so closely

related to logic that every reputable work on logic contains a chapter on ambiguity. He quotes C. Johnston who, in *Chrysal*, published in 1768, wrote: *"I have often been apprehensive, that the manner in which I express myself, may lead you into some mistake of meaning, the signification of words, in the language of man, being so unsettled, that it is scarce possible to convey a determinate sense. . .; for where different, or perhaps contrary meanings are signified by the same word, how easy is it for a mind, prone to error, to take the wrong one."*

However, ambiguity may be used creatively as an individual seeking to understand an ambiguous message is likely to search for the meaning within his own **map of the world** and experience. The process of understanding the different meanings offered may open up choices within the **deep structure** or **unconscious** level.
[See *Transderivational Search*]

ANALOGUE
Submodalities may be intermittent or continuous. An example of the former, in a visual context, might be "light" or "dark"; the latter, for which we use the description *analogue*, could be represented in a kinaesthetic context by, for example, "hard", "moderately hard", or "soft", when describing pressure. An *analogue variable* is anything that can be changed gradually, such as size, brightness, and distance. Body language, facial expression, voice tone are easily recognisable forms of analogical communication; the opposite, ***digital*** communication, is represented by language.

ANALOGY
[See Metaphors]

ANCHORING
The process whereby a (normally external) representation becomes linked to and triggers a response or memory thereby introducing a new dimension into a sensory system. Thus a piece of music may restimulate feelings associated with a particular person or place.

Advertising makes use of anchors to produce a stimulus every time a particular symbol is seen, or by the repetition of a phrase or jingle. The Pavlovian concept of the conditioned reflex is an example of anchoring.

Anchors may be used to construct personal ***resources***. If you were to ask someone to describe how they would like to be, and get a congruent [See ***Congruence***] response of "I don't know...", they could be asked to guess, or imagine, or even invent a response which could then be anchored. This would provide a permanent triggering mechanism to access the resource whenever it was needed. Touching the person's knee or hand for example, at the appropriate moment, would be an appropriate anchoring technique.

Anchors are a means of changing a negative response pattern into a positive response pattern.

Anchoring your own positive resources or, better yet,

having someone assist you to anchor them, is a potent and powerful technique for making a past *state of excellence* available to deal with a present situation. The technique consists of recalling the past state when you were at your most effective, or happiest, or at a peak of vivid experience - whichever you wish to replicate. You then recall what you saw, what you heard, and what you felt at that time. You can imagine yourself within the experience (*associated*), or as if viewing the experience on a cinema screen (*dissociated*), and can make the sight brighter, or turn the sound up louder, or exaggerate the feelings until they are at their most intense.

That condition, the feeling of effectiveness, or happiness, or fulfilment, can then be replicated visually, kinaesthetically or auditorily, or, indeed, by a combination of any or all of them. A visual anchor would consist of seeing something "in your mind's eye" at the peak of experience, which you would recall at such time as you wished to recapture that feeling. A kinaesthetic anchor could be a tap on the knee, or a finger touching your arm, or clasping your hands together. An auditory anchor could be a sound, a word, a phrase, a piece of music.

For an anchor to be effective it must be precisely repeatable. For example, when touching a person to trigger a kinaesthetic anchor, similar pressure must be applied to exactly the location where the anchor was first set up.

Bandler and **Grinder**, in fact, consider kinaesthetic anchoring such as touching to be the most effective, but they have also described a visual anchor:

"So I said "Well, I'd like to speak to that part directly." That always gets [them]. *They don't have that in their model. Then I look over their left shoulder while I talk to them, and that really drives them nuts. But it's a very effective anchoring mechanism, because from that time on, every time you look over their left shoulder, only that part can hear."*[2] [Sometimes referred to as **Linking**. See also *Collapsing Anchors*]

ANCHORS
[See *Anchoring*]

A^r
A symbol representing Auditory Remembered: an internally generated sound associated with a memory.
[See *TOTE notation*]

"AS-IF" FRAME
Acting as if a fictitious event had actually occurred, enabling us to proceed to a desired mental end without being hung-up on imagined difficulties.

A powerful exercise for helping us to identify our ***outcome*** is to imagine ourselves ten years (or ten minutes!) in the future and access our ***sensory systems*** to see, hear and feel what has happened in the intervening period.
[See *Future Pacing*]

ASSOCIATION
Being inside an experience; participating fully through our own senses. Experiencing something as if we are actually there.
[See *Dissociation, First Position*]

A^t
A symbol representing Auditory Tonal: the pitch and timbre of a remembered or uttered sound.
[See *TOTE Notation*]

AUDITORY
Pertaining to the sense of hearing. In NLP terminology it includes our "inner voice".
[See *Internal Auditory Dialogue*]

AUDITORY TAPES
Internal messages, often of a negative, critical nature. "Put-downs". "I'm always wrong." "I'm never successful, so what's the point of trying?" There are NLP exercises which enable these messages to be made less pernicious, or for more useful messages to be substituted.
[See *State*]

AUTHENTICITY
[See *Congruence*]

BACKTRACKING
Repeating or summarising a person's key words, and using the same vocal tone, tempo and volume as the other person, as a method of giving feedback.
[See *Matching*]

BANDLER, RICHARD
One of the founders of NLP in the early seventies, at which time he was a student of psychology at the University of California in Santa Cruz. His collaboration there with **John**

Grinder led to the development of NLP.
[Works include: *Frogs Into Princes* (with John Grinder), *Transformations* (with John Grinder), *Reframing* (with John Grinder) *Magic in Action*, *The Structure of Magic* (two volumes, with John Grinder), *Patterns of the Hypnotic Techniques of Milton H Erickson* (two volumes, with John Grinder), *Using Your Brain For a Change*]
[See *Neuro Linguistic Programming*]

BATESON, GREGORY
British anthropologist and expert on *cybernetics*, who applied the cybernetic approach to his studies of biology, psychotherapy and anthropology. His theories had a profound influence on the development of **Family Therapy** as well as on **Richard Bandler** and **John Grinder** who pioneered NLP.
[Works include: *Mind and Nature* and *Steps to an Ecology of Mind*]
[See *Neuro Linguistic Programming*]

BATNA
Acronym standing for *Best Alternative to a Negotiated Agreement*. An outcome decided through a process of *future pacing* which will be acceptable to an individual, even though agreement has not been reached. The purpose of a BATNA is to increase the flexibility of a negotiator. In effect the BATNA removes from the mind of one party the condition that a negotiation must be concluded with an agreement. This serves to change the rules of the negotiation in the favour of this individual.

BEHAVIOUR
Human activity, both physical and mental: the actions and reactions through which we interact with the people and the environment around us. One of the six neurological levels of **Robert Dilts' unified field theory**.
  Behaviour in NLP is regarded as an important part of

communication, and non-verbal responses are at least as significant as words. As the old saw has it: "Actions speak louder than words".

BEHAVIOURAL DEMONSTRATION
Specific, observable ongoing examples of *vital signs*.
[See *Sensory Acuity*]

BELIEF CHANGE PATTERN
A program for change described by ***Richard Bandler***[3] which comprises three main processes: (a) the gathering and preparation of information; (b) the belief change process; and (c) testing the result.

In (a) the subject thinks of a belief they have about themselves which they would like to change, examines the way they represent it internally, considers something they doubt, then examines and lists the *submodality* differences between the two, and establishes a new belief they would like in place of the disliked belief.

In (b) the subject changes the unwanted belief to doubt, using a powerful submodality, changes the content of the old belief to the new one by using another submodality, then, keeping the new content, changes doubt to belief by reversing the submodality used originally.

Finally (c) is the process of checking out how one feels about the new belief.

BELIEF SYSTEM
A patterning of the mind relating to cause, meaning and boundaries in our environment, our behaviour, our capabilities or our identities. If we receive the message that we are unlikely or unable to do something, the chances are that our mind will reinforce such a belief and we will not be able to do it. On the other hand, if our nervous system feeds our brains with congruent (See *Congruence*) messages that something is within our power to achieve, then we will almost certainly achieve it.

Thus, if we can model another person's belief system, it is more likely we can achieve the same results as the person being modelled. This is how we follow cookery recipes.

Examples of limiting belief tend to fall into one or more of three categories: *hopelessness*, *helplessness* and *worthlessness*.
[See *Conceptual Modelling*]

BELIEFS
Generalisations which we make about the world, and those principles by which we function in it.

BLAMER
A caricature of an individual who makes **visual** (***V***) comparisons and becomes angry when what is seen does not accord with the perfection anticipated.
[See *Satir, Virginia*]

BODY LANGUAGE
We communicate not only with words, but also with our bodies: our gestures, our postures, our facial expressions, our breathing, our tone of voice. We fail to communicate adequately when, for instance, the message we intend to convey with our words fails to get across to the person to whom it is addressed. The problem may lie in the ***incongruency*** of our words and our body language. Our words may say one thing, while the other person may be picking up a totally different message from our posture or our tone.
[See *Congruence, Incongruence*]

BREAK STATE
Returning a person to the 'here and now' for the purpose of separating ***state*** elicited during ***anchoring***. This ensures that the ***Four-Tuple*** associated with a specific anchor remains separate from the four-tuple or state associated with other experiences.

BREATHING
The most important indicator of an individual's internal state. It is a more reliable pointer to the sensory system than, for example, **eye movements**, as changes in breathing are more consistent than eye movements in determining an individual's sensory state.

BREATHING PATTERNS
Shallow breathing in the upper chest responds to the **Visual** sensory system. Even rhythmic breathing in the mid-chest area indicates an **Auditory** sensory state. Deep breathing from the abdomen suggests **Kinaesthetic** sensory feelings.

 Knowing how our breathing patterns respond to a particular sensory system can enable us to use them as a resource. For example, when we are nervous or anxious, our breathing becomes shallow; deep breathing at such a time may help to correct our condition. How often have we told someone, or been told, to "take a couple of deep breaths"?

CALIBRATED LOOP
A circular process where two or more people pair each others unconscious, non-verbal responses and associate observable behaviour with their specific internal responses.
[See *Accessing Cues, Anchoring, Cause-Effect*].

CALIBRATION
The ability to interpret non-verbal messages and to associate them with a person's internal state. Calibration is essential to good communication and can involve the study of eye movements, posture, facial expression, and breathing.

 Certain types of questions may be used to determine an internal state, by observing eye movements, even when no verbal answer is given. The following descriptions apply in most cases. They refer to what you might see as an observer with the subject facing you, or when looking at yourself in a mirror.

(a) To induce visual remembered response:

What was written on the spine of the last book you read?
What colour is your front door?
What does your favourite skirt/tie look like?
[*Eyes would move upper right*]
(b) To induce visual construct response:
How would you look with a beard/pony tail/bald head?
How would you look falling down a mountain side?
What would you look like as you approached a black hole?
[*Eyes would move upper left*]
(c) To induce auditory remembered response:
What does your favourite song sound like?
What does a cello sound like?
What was the special quality of the nicest voice you ever heard?
[*Eyes would move to the right side*]
(d) To induce auditory construct response:
How would you sound if you tried to mimic a gorilla?
How would you sound with a man's/woman's voice?
[*Eyes would move to the left side*]
(e) To induce auditory internal dialogue:
Try to hear yourself describing your work to someone.
Ask yourself the question: "What is my main ambition?".
What would be your statement if you were asked to sum up the Palestinian issue?
[*Eyes would move down to the right*]
(f) To induce a kinaesthetic response:
What does suede leather feel like?
How does it feel to sink into a soft, warm bed?
How does champagne taste?
[*Eyes would move down to the left*]
[See *Accessing Cues* and *TOTE notation*]

CAPABILITY
Our ability successfully to perform a task, our strategy, and our perception of it.

CASTANEDA, CARLOS
A former UCLA student of anthropology and the author of books on Shamanism. His works are cited in transcripts of Bandler and Grinder's early workshops and his ideas influenced *New Code NLP*.
[See: *Bandler, Richard, Grinder, John* and *Magic*]

CATASTROPHES
Past traumas and negative *imprints* from *personal history*.
[See *Seven C's Model*]

CAUSE AND EFFECT
Making a connection between a perception and an experience, or between two experiences. When such a generalisation is not useful it may be challenged using the *Meta Model*, whereby an act, statement, or facial expression of one person has an effect on the emotional state of another, and the second person may reveal this through a cause-effect statement. Thus: "You annoy me," or "My work irritates me." Typical meta-model responses might be: "What exactly annoys you about my behaviour?" or "How specifically does your work irritate you?"
[See *Anchoring* for a fuller understanding of how cause and effect patterns are first established]

CAUSES
The *deep structure* responsible for creating and maintaining the symptoms. As these are at a deeper level they are less obvious than the symptoms themselves which have been modelled into a *surface structure*.
[See *SCORE Model*]

CHAINING ANCHORS
Creating a link between a specific stimulus and a desired response:
1. A *problem state* is elicited, *calibrated* and an anchor set up for it.

2. The person is reoriented back into the present; the *break state*.
3. An *outcome state* is elicited and anchored.
4. A further break state is introduced.
5. The first anchor is triggered.
6. At the first sign that the individual is accessing (but not fully immersed), in the problem state the second anchor is triggered and held; the first anchor is then released before the problem state has reached it's threshold.
7. The pattern is tested by introducing a break state and then firing the first anchor. If the pattern has been set up adequately this should elicit the outcome state.
[See also A*nchors; Collapsing Anchors*]

CHANGING PERSONAL HISTORY

This is a technique for editing our memories, particularly those memories which cause us pain, or which we tend to blame for any repetitious, negative behaviour or feelings. In effect we re-write a movie script, in which we are a participant, to give it a happier (or more satisfying) narrative than it had in the original version. Because our feelings in the present are often based on faulty memories of past events, we can change our present feelings by re-evaluating the memories on which they are based. The technique is:
1. Identify the painful memory or experience that you would like to change.
2. Have someone calibrate the negative state, then anchor it (for example, by touching a spot on your arm).
3. Check that the negative anchor is installed. **Break state**.
4. Elicit a new script, based on present-time experience and knowledge, which would have been more desirable, happier, or more satisfying.
5. Install a positive anchor, possibly by touching a spot on the other arm. Test the anchor. Break state.
6. Return to the memory or experience that you desire to change and view it as on a cinema screen (see *Dissociated*) while the positive anchor is still in place. Notice how the

altered perceptions and the addition of present-time resources have changed the experience. Then, still holding the positive anchor, step into the picture as a participant (see ***associated***) and relive the experience utilising present-time positive responses and knowledge.

7. Repeat the last three steps, if necessary, until satisfied that a new, more satisfying, script has been established. If any difficulty is encountered in achieving this, go back to step 4 and stack resources, i.e. reinforce your state by adding further resources or experiences, effectively piling one resource on top of another.

8. The new response pattern is now established. Recall of the past experience will no longer elicit the same feelings.
[See *Anchors, Calibration, Collapsing Anchors, Resourceful States, Resources, Timelines*]

CHOMSKY NOAM

American linguist, writer, educator and political activist. Considered to be responsible for the development of ***transformational grammar***. The influence of his work undoubtedly contributed to the development of the ***Meta-Model*** from which NLP was developed.
Works include: *Syntactic Structures (1957), in which he sets out his theory of transformational grammar. Cartesian Linguistics (1966); Language and the Mind (1968); Language and Responsibility (1979);* and, *Language and the Problems of Knowledge (1988).*

CHUNKING

This is a term taken from computer terminology, where it means breaking things into bits. In NLP it means organising information into suitable sizes or "chunks" so that it can be easily absorbed.

"Chunking down" involves breaking a large body of information into smaller chunks so that they can be more comfortably studied or understood. "Chunking up" occurs when all the smaller parts are tied together and placed in the

WHAT ARE YOU SCULPTING?
AN ELEPHANT
THAT MUST BE DIFFICULT
NO, I JUST CHIP AWAY EVERYTHING WHICH DOESN'T LOOK LIKE AN ELEPHANT
?

context of the total subject being considered.

Whenever a proposition appears too difficult to be mastered, chunking down will enable you to drop to a level where it is no longer too complex or overwhelming. (Thus: "How do you sculpt an elephant?" "One chip at a time.") Someone learning to drive a car will first learn the individual skills of handling the clutch, steering, reading the dashboard instruments, understanding traffic signs and the highway code. Once these are mastered, the learner can then chunk up to the actual process of driving.

George Miller in *The Magical Number Seven, Plus or Minus Two* (1956) demonstrated that people can deal with no more than seven chunks of information (plus or minus two) consciously and comfortably. More than nine chunks of information overloads the mind at which point conscious awareness gives way to trance. Less than five chunks is inefficient.

[Also known as *Stepping*]

COLLAPSING ANCHORS

This is a technique of dealing with a problem state by linking a positive *anchor* to a negative anchor which, after a period of *confusion*, results in the positive anchor predominating. It works in the following way.

1. The problem state is identified and accessed through the primary senses, so that you re-experience all the sights, sounds, and feelings associated with that state. When these are totally experienced a negative anchor is set up by touching a part of your body..
2. Break out of the state [See **Break State**] and test the negative anchor by applying the same touch, and make sure that it recalls the problem state. Break state again.
3. Think of a positive state you would prefer to have and access all the sights, sounds and feelings you can associate with that state. When you are experiencing that state most intensely, set up a positive anchor by touching yourself on another part of your body.

4. Break out of the positive state. Then ensure that you can recapture the positive state by applying the positive anchor. If you have any difficulty in achieving this, go back into the state and make the sights clearer and brighter, the sounds louder, the feelings more intense. If they seem to have significance, add your memories of smells or tastes associated with the experience.

5. Taking care to break the state between each test and before proceeding to step 6. Check both anchors again to make sure they activate the two separate responses.

6. Trigger both anchors simultaneously and observe the unusual, even dramatic, effect until - in theory, and if the collapsing anchors exercise has succeeded - the positive state response has gained the upper hand.

7. If the positive state response does not offset the negative state response pattern, or does not do so quickly enough, you may need to stack positive resource anchors. This involves adding further resources or experiences to the anchors, in effect piling one anchor on top of another.

The result of this will be to set up a resource state for use whenever you need or want it, and provides the ability to change an unwanted negative pattern into a desired and positive state of resourcefulness.

[See *Chaining Anchors, Resourceful State*]

COMBINING LINKS
[See *Links*]

COMMUNICATION
The process of conveying information, ideas, or intention, by language, signs, symbols and behaviour.

What is said is less important than the way it is said. If a communication is *incongruent* and results in a response which is different from what was expected, it suggests that *rapport* has not been achieved with the other person, and a variation of the form of communication will be useful. *Language* is generally a poor form of communication unless it is translated into the ***representational system*** of the other person. ***Behaviour*** is a far more effective form of communication

Gregory Bateson distinguishes between ***content*** and ***relationship*** messages in human communication. What a person says constitutes the content message of the communication; what a person does non-verbally constitutes the relationship message. The latter, using representations such as gestures and grimaces, is described as analogic communication; the former, using language, is described as digital communication. *"It would seem that analogic communication is in some sense more primitive than digital and that there is a broad evolutionary trend towards the substitution of digital for analogic mechanisms in higher mammals."*[4]

Communication on one level encourages response on the same level. We tend to interact with others according to the perceived message we are getting from them. A behavioural

pattern in you will induce certain behaviour in me. Your use of words may elicit my use of words. My response will key your response. We nevertheless have the option of changing our choice of communication process, and this could have the result of improving understanding and *rapport*. It is important to watch, listen and pay attention to all the cues you receive from the person with whom you are communicating. However, because so much is occurring in every interaction, this paying attention is usually divorced from *conscious awareness*.

Virginia Satir : *"If you did nothing more when you have a family together than to make it possible for them to really look at each other, really touch each other, and listen to each other, you would already have swung the pendulum in the direction of a new start."*[5]
[See also *Accessing Cues, Calibrated Loop, Congruence, Language, Third Position, Unconscious Mind*]

COMPARISONS
An element in the *Meta Model* typified by the use of such words as *"better"*, *"worse"*, *"harder"*, *"easier"*. As with other meta model patterns, comparisons are dealt with by a request for specificity. "Better than what?" "Better than whom?" "Compared with what?"
[See also: *Seven C's Model*]

COMPLEMENTARY RELATIONSHIPS
Refers to those relationships in which the more A performs a behaviour, the less B will perform the same or similar behaviour. For example, if A becomes aggressive, B will become more calm and reassuring. This will cause A to become more aggressive resulting in B becoming even more calm. If B changes behaviour and challenges A, then A will begin to behave in a calmer manner.
[See *Symmetrical Relationships*]

COMPLEX EQUIVALENCE

A *non sequitur*. "You are not smiling" *ergo* "you are unhappy". Linking any two such statements produces a complex equivalence.

This involves **generalisation** because it is usually based on one's own experience. If my thought processes are visual, I am likely to link the actions of a kinaesthetic person in a complex equivalence, e.g. *You are not looking at me* will equate with *You are not paying attention*, even though I may not usually be aware of my complex equivalence.

The existence of a complex equivalence is generally a sign that the person is trapped in their own **model of the world**, since the words a person uses are associated with different internal experiences than those of other people.
[See *Meta Model, Sleight of Mouth Patterns*]

COMPUTER

Pejorative term for a person who thinks in word concepts.
[See A^d, *Satir, Virginia*]

CONCEPTUAL MODELLING

A style of modelling created by **Robert Dilts** in order to discover the mental map which determined the thinking processes of historical and fictional individuals. This is different from the approach adopted by **Bandler** and **Grinder** in the original modelling projects which led to the creation of NLP.

Conceptual modelling concentrates on beliefs and values, and states and strategies, and tends to be inferred rather than observed directly through the five senses. This opens up the possibility of modelling the strategies of such seminal figures as: Aristotle, Einstein, Freud, Leonardo da Vinci and Mozart.
[See also *Logical Levels, Modelling*]

CONFLICT

[See *Incongruence; Secondary Gain* and *Seven C's Model*]

CONFUSION

We all know more than we think we do; our comprehension is only limited by our failure to organise the data we possess.

IF I BECOME... ...WELL ADJUSTED

PEOPLE WON'T NOTICE... ...HOW CONFUSED I AM

   Richard Bandler makes the point that it is usually having too much rather than too little information which causes confusion. *"Confusion,"* he says *"is always an indication that you're on your way to understanding."*[3] One way to enable ourselves to organise the information we already have is by ***chunking***.
[See *Seven C's Model*]

CONGRUENCE
That situation wherein we use all our communicative aspects,

such as words, tonality, and body language, to express the same message, suggesting that we are totally unified and sincere in seeking an **outcome**. When I am not congruent my behaviour and my words may often give different messages: I may say one thing and do another. Congruency exists when all of our **output channels** convey the same or compatible messages.

Congruence not only implies authenticity; an individual who is congruent will inspire confidence and trust in others. All that person's internal beliefs, strategies and behaviours are fully in agreement and directed toward a purposeful outcome. Consequently if I wish to influence others, I will achieve greater impact if I can achieve congruency, where all my parts are unified in working towards my outcome.
[See *C-Operator, Incongruence*]

CONNECTEDNESS
The desire or requirement to feel that we belong. Believing that we are related to others, finding a partner, identifying with a group, satisfying these needs, helps us to know who we are and to feel connected.

CONSCIOUS
Existing in present moment awareness.
[See also *First Attention, Unconscious, Uptime* and *Downtime*]

CONSTITUENT STRUCTURE
In linguistics, a judgement about the constitution of an appropriate unit within a sentence. The constituent structure of a sentence is assigned by the rules that generate the sentence.
[See *Transformational Grammar* and *Chomsky, Noam*]

CONSTRAINTS
[See *Perceptual Filters*]

CONSTRUCTIVIST
One who applies the constructivist philosophy that experience is constructed via culture, language and narrative from signals received and filtered by the nervous system. Experience is therefore never direct, but relies on a constructed internal map which is mistaken for reality itself. NLP is therefore a constructivist discipline.
[See *Map of the World*]

CONTENT
The ***digital***, or ***narrative*** ingredient of a communication.
[See *Seven C's Model*]

CONTENT REFRAMING
Taking a situation and changing its meaning. Giving an alternative meaning to a statement which may suggest an unpleasant or unsatisfactory ***outcome***, such as "We're not retreating, we're advancing in another direction". The inability to perform a task, or the fear of failing in its performance, could be reframed by asking: "What else might this mean?" or "What benefit might I obtain from avoiding this task?" Or, putting it another way: "If at first you don't succeed, redefine success."
[See *Reframing*]

CONTEXT
A physical or psychological space defining the rules in which an event's meaning may be understood.
[See *Seven C's Model*]

CONTEXT MARKER
Meta messages which define the boundaries of a context. Someone entering a building will be influenced in their behaviour within the building by virtue of the ritual by which they are invited inside as well as by markers within the building itself. If we are not offered a chair; or if our host sits on a dais and looks down upon us, we are more likely to

defer to those who customarily occupy the property. If, on entering, however, chairs are arranged in a circle and a few people are already sitting, then the context as marked by the chairs, is likely to be one of equality.

The incidental removal of a context marker may upset the delicate balance of how we relate to our immediate community or family. For example when smoking rooms are removed from offices, the smokers from different departments are no longer able to exchange information about their quadrants of the parent organisation so co-operation in the building as a whole becomes more fragmented. Similarly family members who use the opportunity to smoke as the signal to make plans for family finances, education or holidays may find that planning goes awry until a new context for these discussions is marked.

CONTEXT REFRAMING
Seeking an alternative place where a difficult behaviour might be more appropriate. The compulsion to perform an

unwelcome behaviour in a particular situation could be reframed by asking: "Where would it be more beneficial to do this?" The salesman who reported to his boss that "We cannot sell our shoes here; everyone goes barefooted," could reframe to: "Nobody here has shoes; what a wonderful opportunity for our product."
[See *Reframing*]

CONTROLLER
A *part* created or operating at a high logical level the function of which is to preserve the ecology of a system, (or person).
[See *Demon State, New Code NLP.*]

CONVERSATIONAL POSTULATE
Putting a command in the form of a question. "Are the dishes still on the table?" is not asking for a yes or no reply, but in effect is saying: "Do the washing up."

CONVICTION
[See *Seven C's Model*]

C-OPERATOR
The C- or Congruency Operator is a way of describing and notating how much of the expression of any moment of time is congruent [See ***Congruence***] within all of the five senses.

Understanding the limits of consciousness is important both in the application of ***Modelling, Hypnosis*** and ***NLP Psychotherapy***. When information is not represented consciously (see ***R-Operator.***), the ***unconscious*** understanding may communicate itself out of an individual's conscious awareness. When the message is congruent across all of the five senses then the C-operator is notated as 'Yes'. When there is ***incongruence*** it is notated as 'No'.
[See *Four Tuple, R-Operator, Tote Notation, Tracking*]

CORE TRANSFORMATION
Attributed in NLP to Connirae Andreas[6]. The Core is the

wellspring from which all perceptions arise. Often denied, the Core Transformation Process is designed to reunite anindividual with one of five core states: Being; Peace; Love; OK-ness and Oneness.

The structure of the process is as follows:
1. Identify something you would like to achieve and give it a name, such as purchasing a new car.
2. Ask yourself: if you had the car what would you See, Hear, Feel. Fully associate into the experience.
3. From within the experience ask yourself what would give you even more satisfaction, and give it a name. . . .
4. Go back to stage 2. repeating as many times as needed until a core state is reached.
5. Name your core state and establish an *anchor* for it.
6. From being associated in the core state go back down through all the stages in reverse order asking yourself: "Now that I experience my core state how does this change my experience of, (for example) purchasing a new car?
7. Process each stage gaining insight about yourself and your life until you have attached the core state to all your ambitions and or challenges.

The process may be adapted to working therapeutically with illnesses, as well as with those seeking self fulfilment. [See: *Spirit*]

CRITERIA

Values that are important in a specific context. Criteria are the determinants of why we do certain things: they largely govern our relationships, our leisure pursuits, our work.

If we shared the same values and the same priorities as everyone else, we would find life a lot simpler. In interacting with others it is useful, therefore, to establish our own and their **hierarchy of values** and **hierarchy of criteria**. Criteria respond to the questions: What motivates me? What is important to me? What do I really want from life?

[See *Values*]

CROSS-OVER MIRRORING
Mirroring consists of matching another person's verbal and non-verbal behaviour for the purpose of establishing **rapport** with that person. Language and body posture can be mirrored, as can breathing, voice tone and tempo, facial expression, etc.

On the non-verbal level, direct mirroring is the precise duplication of such behaviour as rate and depth of breathing. But it is also possible to mirror non-verbally by substituting one non-verbal channel for another. This is what is called *cross-over mirroring*. For instance, one person can match the nodding of their head to the tempo of another's breathing. It can be done very subtly, yet can be as powerful as direct mirroring. In this example, we have cross-over mirroring in the same channel, namely the kinaesthetic mode.

Cross-over mirroring can also be effected by switching channels.

If I match the tempo of my speech to the pattern of another's breathing, then I am mirroring their kinaesthetic behaviour in the verbal channel.
[See *Leading, Matching, Pacing, Switching*]

CYBERNETICS
The study of self-teaching systems. Derived from the Greek *kybernetikos* ("good at steering") and credited to the mathematician Norbert Wiener as the founder of the field as an independent science.

Within a cybernetic system an individual component or subsystem, when seeking to complete a task, will vary its behaviour and/or set intermediate goals. Any obstacle encountered, will comprise opportunities for learning which may be utilised in the further stages towards accomplishing the task.

Learning, in cybernetics, is achieved by the process of negative feedback. This is not punishment; rather it is the process of continuous **mapping** during the non-achievement of **outcomes**. This non-achievement constitutes difference arising from the tension between effort (or operation) and result. Instant achievement involves no new information, and therefore no new learning. [See Bateson, Gregory [4]]

As learning increases, the component may gain sufficient self-referring knowledge to enable the structure of some of the lower levels of the system to be varied, in order more efficiently to complete the task. This is called self-development or self-improvement.

It is likely that much of the organisation of the human brain is patterned on the basis of self-teaching and self-development and, by comparison, minimally constrained by genetic factors.

In NLP the statements: *"There is no such thing as failure, only feedback"* and *"If what you are doing is not working, do something else"* are both rooted in the science of cybernetics.
[See *Family Therapy, Presuppositions of NLP*]

DECISION POINT
The moment of choice as to which technique to follow in aiding a subject to achieve a specific **outcome**.
[See also: *TOTE* and *TOTE Notation*]

DEEP STRUCTURE
Our deepest linguistic representation of what we want to say. It is rooted in the unconscious, and tends to be too complex for everyday communication, and so is simplified to **surface structure** in conversation. **Bandler** and **Grinder**[7] describe it as "the full linguistic representation from which the surface structures of the language are derived."

Our deep structure comprises the totality of our experiences of the world. Within the realms of perception, deep structure and surface structure, our representations are affected by the three processes of **generalisation**, **deletion**, and **distortion** through which we create our **model of the world**.
[See *Meta Model, Modelling, New Code NLP, Transformational Grammar*]

DELETION

Excluding part of an experience from thought or speech. With over two million pieces of information being fed into the human nervous system every second, we need to use deletion to prevent incoming sensory data from swamping us. Thus we can use deletion to filter out sounds (as, for example, at a cocktail party) when trying to listen to the voice of one person; or, when we are studying, we can delete external sounds from our awareness. People living near the railway track ultimately fail to hear the noise of the passing trains.

George Miller in his paper "The Magical Number Seven Plus or Minus Two...", has described how the human mind is able to retain only seven (plus or minus two) pieces of information in consciousness. As you read these words, you may be aware of the type of print, the content of each sentence, the temperature of the room, the intensity of the light, the chair you are sitting on. If you had to be consciously aware of all this information plus the rate at which your heart is beating, the sounds outside the room, the pressure of your shoe against your foot, the objects within your peripheral vision, the blink of your eyes as you take another breath, you would become too overwhelmed to function.

So deletion enables us to function with conscious awareness.

It is not always an advantage, however, to exclude an original experience from our internal representation. We sometime block ourselves from hearing important messages, thereby causing ourselves or others pain.

With the process of deletion parts of the **deep structure** are removed from *surface structure* representations.
[See *Chunking, Seven - The Magical Number*]

DELOZIER, Judith
Co-author with Richard Bandler, John Grinder and Robert Dilts of *Neuro-Linguistic Programming*: Volume I, *The Study of the Structure of Subjective Experience* (1980); with John Grinder of *Turtles All the Way Down* (1987); and with John Grinder and Charlotte Bretto of *Leaves Before the Wind* (1990).

DEMON OR DEMON STATE
An autonomous part created to complete a specific function, such as writing a book. Within New Code NLP a controller is also set up at a higher logical level than the demons, the controller's function being to mediate between conflicting demons, and to monitor the ecology of the individual and his environment. For example to ensure that the individual does his/her share of the washing up and thus does not lose the respect of their partner.

DESIRED STATE
A positive physiological/psychological state, normally

indicating that an individual is functioning in a *state of excellence*, or that state in which a person wants to be functioning: journey's end for a well-formed outcome.
[See *Outcome, Well-formed*]

DIGITAL [Also Discontinuous]
The opposite of *analogue* which, between limits, can vary continuously, digital variable such as black or white, on or off, associated or dissociated, is a *submodality* which has to be one thing or another, and cannot be both at the same time. Language is digital communication.

When used to describe a person, digital has the same meaning as *computer*.
[See *Analogues, Satir, Virginia*]

DILTS, ROBERT
Early collaborator with *Richard Bandler* and *John Grinder* at the University of California in Santa Cruz. Co-author with Richard Bandler, John Grinder, and Judith DeLozier of *Neuro-Linguistic Programming*: Volume I (1980). His *unified field* model was a significant contribution to NLP. Other works include *Applications of Neuro-Linguistic Programming, Belief Systems and Your Well-being*, and *Roots of Neuro-Linguistic Programming, Strategies of Genius* - (currently 3 volumes); and (with Roberto Bonissone) *Skills for the Future*.

DISASSOCIATION [See Dissociation]

DISCONTINUOUS [See Digital]

DISNEY STRATEGY
According to *Robert Dilts*, Walt Disney employed a strategy for success wherein his first three perceptual positions were specialised in the following ways:
First Position: A visionary dreamer who literally pictures all the elements in a project.

Second Position: The ability to enter into the narrative of the project in an associated way and feel all the emotions and elements involved.

Third Position: A dissociated critic, named by Dilts as 'the spoiler', who looks for problems in the project and criticises them, in much the same way as a bank manager might.

Creativity takes place via co-operative communication between these three positions. Disney's specialised way of being creative differs slightly from the way in which first, second and third position are often attributed. This arises because his "dreamer", or first position is dissociated, *through time* into the future.

[See: *Triple description*]

DISSOCIATION [Also known as Disassociation]

Being outside an experience; seeing it as an observer rather than as a participant. As if seeing yourself in a film. A technique often used to enable an individual to avoid experiencing difficult or painful feelings.

[See *Association*]

DISTORTION

An inaccurate internal representation which allows sensory data to be rearranged. Distortion is the way we alter our perceptions and, by helping us to fantasise, helps us to model the world. It also enables us to prepare for experiences before they occur, but by the same token may contribute to our mistaken belief that our model is the real world.

It is responsible for quantum leaps both in understanding and in misunderstanding, and is part of the process of creativity, but by the same token can result, in extreme cases, in chronic psychiatric disorders.

Thus, while we may never dream of eating the menu when we want the meal, we may metaphorically fall into precisely that trap by mistaking our personal map of the world for the actual territory.

To a great extent, *generalisation* and *deletion* are extensions of distortion.

The process of distortion within language systems is known as **nominalization**.

[See *Constructivism, Modelling, Model of the World*]

DISTRACTER
A caricature of a person who is influenced by sound and as a result is attracted to where there is most auditory stimulation. Sometimes referred to by Satir as the Irrelevant One[8]. This person is likely to engage in other peoples conversations, gossip and be unable to keep to any one task. However they can appear to be quite self absorbed and may sometimes be found humming, or singing to themselves.

[See *Satir, Virginia*]

DOMINANT SENSORY SYSTEM
That sensory system most commonly employed by an individual to process information, indicated habitually by **predicate patterns** and **eye accessing cues**.

[See *Representational Systems*]

DOVETAILING OUTCOMES
The process of accommodating or matching different **outcomes** so that neither party loses as, for example, in the art of **negotiation**. It incorporates the art of influencing without manipulating, achieving **rapport**, and respecting the other's integrity while maintaining your own.

Conflicts occur because we have different **models of the world**, yet we may have similar **outcomes** which we fail to recognise through poor **communication**. Dovetailing occurs when we can find areas of agreement enabling our models of the world to overlap, so that we each understand better the point of view of the other.

[See *Manipulation*]

DOWNTIME
Focusing inwards to our own thoughts and feelings. Being in a trance-like state as a result of being totally immersed in our internal level. Looking inward for solutions or memories.
[See *Uptime, Transderivational Search*]

DRAGON STATE
A *state* that you and others can do without. The opposite of resourceful empowering states.
[See *Resourceful State*; *Seven Cs model*]

ECOLOGY
Regard for the relationship between living creatures and their environment. Internal ecology in NLP refers to the relationship a person has with himself and the environment of which he is a part, as represented by his pattern of values, strategies, and behaviours. An ecological check is one of our tests of the authenticity of our well-formed outcomes.
[See *Congruence, New Code NLP, Outcomes, Well-formed*]

EFFECT
The purpose or result of a step. Generally to access, organise or evaluate. The second 'test' within a ***TOTE***. These results or responses to the achievement of an ***outcome*** should not be mistaken for the outcome itself.
[See *Well-Formedness, SCORE, Model*]

EFFERENT TRACK
[See *New Code NLP*]

ELEGANCE PRINCIPLE
A principle of modelling which states that only those elements necessary to the performance of the task need be learned. Superfluous characteristics of the person modelled are best discarded as they are likely to be associated with other ***parts*** of that person and may conflict with parts of the modeller.

ELICITATION
Gathering information by direct observation of an individual's non-verbal signals, and asking questions designed to test their internal experience structure; e.g. **meta model** questions; and can also be used to direct the subject into a desired emotional state. In everyday life we attempt to do this when we "try to make someone feel better".

An example of a question designed to elicit a resourceful emotional state might be: "Do you remember a time when you succeeded at what you did not expect to achieve?"

EMPRINT METHOD
[See *Mental Aptitude Patterning*]

ENNEAGRAM
Not strictly NLP but integrated by some into an NLP framework. The Enneagram is an ancient system of categorisation that proposes nine basic personality types. These are: Achiever, Helper, Succeeder, Individualist, Observer, Guardian, Dreamer, Confronter and Preservationist.

The Enneagram is a tool for assessing human personality. It is also a tool for flexible problem solving.

The value of the Enneagram is its ability to help you solve your everyday problems. It enables you to make decisions. It does not provide the answer, but it will suggest answers and will help to clarify the question and expose the consequences of any course of action. It will provide insights which you might otherwise fail to appreciate. One of its many advantages is its flexibility.

ENGRAM
A stabilised pattern which is automatic. For example: putting your foot on the brake pedal when you approach a red light. The problem with engrams is that they offer no choice. In the case of braking at a red light, the response is a useful one; failure to achieve the level of *unconscious competence*

[See *Learning, Four Stages of*] in such a situation could lead to a nasty accident. Should the engram involve some form of addictive behaviour, however, the response could be far from useful. Such a situation might arise, for example, if you experience a stomach upset whenever you have to make a journey, or sit an examination, or attend an interview; it might arise if you find yourself incapable of resisting the lure of a box of chocolates despite being overweight.
[See also *Imprint*]

ENTRY CUES
[See *Accessing cues*]

EPISTEMOLOGY
Enquiry into the nature, powers and limitations of knowledge; recognising what we know, determining how we know it, and identifying the channels through which knowledge comes, i.e. the senses, the intellect, the intuition, or all three. How do we know that we know? How do you think about thinking? What is the pattern that connects. . .? These are all examples of epistemological questions. NLP is epistemological in its application.
[See *Bateson Gregory, Ecology and Turtles*]

ERICKSON, MILTON H.
A key figure and leading practitioner in the field of hypnotherapy, whose instinctive abilities and use of non-verbal behaviour patterns caused him to be chosen as one of three major models by ***John Grinder*** and ***Richard Bandler*** in their development of NLP [The other two being ***Fritz Perls*** and ***Virginia Satir***]. *Patterns of Hypnotic Techniques* of Milton H. Erickson, Volume I (1975) was co-authored by Grinder and Bandler, and Volume II (1977) was co-authored by Grinder, Bandler and Judith DeLozier.

In 1954 Erickson published his first paper on the use of Indirect Hypnotic Therapy whereby inducing a trance state in his subject enabled them to access their own resources for solving their problems. His reputation as a therapist derived very much from his instinctive ability to use language and non-verbal means of guiding his clients into an impasse of behaviour and/or thinking, making it easier to get them into a trance state.

Erickson's use of language to induce a trance state in order to access the unconscious resources of the personality was modelled in NLP, and became known as the **Milton Model**.
[Publications include: *Collected Works* (4 Volumes) edited by Ernest L Rossi, *Teachings, Seminars and Workshops* (4 Volumes) edited by Rossi, Ryan and Sharp, *Time Distortion in Hypnosis* (with Lynn Cooper), *The February Man* (Edited by Ernest L Rossi) and *Conversations with Milton H. Erickson* (3 volumes) edited by Jay Haley.]

EXCELLENCE
The possession of good qualities in an unusual degree. NLP has been described as a practical tool for the investigation and duplication of personal excellence.

An exercise sometimes employed in NLP is to work with a partner in replicating a personal state of excellence: confidence, or determination, or optimism, and then compare it with a negative state such as anger or confusion. The exercise demonstrates powerfully the interaction between emotional states and physiological states.
[See *Advanced Modelling Strategy*, *Congruence*, *Seven C's Model*]

EYE ACCESSING CUES
At any particular time involuntary eye movements may indicate which sensory systems are being used. Eye accessing cues is that set of *accessing cues* concerned with how the eyes move and the sequence of positions they adopt. To know how people are accessing information, to deduce strategies and to understand them, it is important to know the internal process to which each position equates.

A person's eye movements will reveal whether they are

running a video picture in their "mind's eye", listening to an internal audio tape, or concentrating on their feelings. An upward movement of the eyes indicates that a person is accessing in the visual mode. If the eyes move upward and to the left, the visualisation is of an actual past event; if the movement is to the right, the visualisation is of something imaginary. A sideways movement of the eyes denotes that a person is accessing the auditory system. Sideways and to the left denotes remembered sounds; sideways and to the right means the person is imagining, or constructing, a sound. When accessing feelings, the eyes will typically go down to the right; when the eyes go down to the left we are engaging in internal dialogue, i.e. talking to ourselves.

The eye movements described above will apply typically to a right handed person. The directions may be reversed for left handed subjects.

Eye accessing cues help us, as do other types of accessing cues, to know how another person is thinking. For some examples of simple questions which enable us to demonstrate accessing cues to identify a persons preferred sensory system see under *Accessing Cues*.

VISUAL REMEMBERED (V^r)   **VISUAL CONSTRUCT (V^c)**

AUDITORY REMEMBERED (A^r) *I still remember her last words*

AUDITORY CONSTRUCT (V^c) *If you were to ask me I'd probably say...*

INNER DIALOGUE (A^id) *Let me just think about that*

KINAESTHETIC (K) *The prospect really excites me*

A kind of "shorthand" known as **TOTE notation** is used to represent the various forms of eye accessing cues. This consists of the following:

V^r = Visual remembered. Visualising images of things previously seen.

V^c = Visual construct.   Seeing images of things imagined.
A^r = Auditory remembered. Hearing sounds previously heard.
A^c Auditory construct.   Imagining sounds never heard before.
A^d = Internal dialogue.   Talking to oneself.
K = Kinaesthetic.   Internal and external feelings.
We can use eye movements to aid us in recalling our own memories, or in accessing a *resourceful state*. If we need to remember a telephone number, for example, and we wish to visualise it in our diary, looking up and to the left may help us to do so. If we are trying to remember a piece of music, looking sideways to the left may help.

EYE ENTRY CUES
[See Eye Accessing Cues]

FAILURE INTO FEEDBACK STRATEGY
A technique developed by **Robert Dilts** and Todd Epstein which makes use of *eye accessing cues* in cases of chronic stuckness or depression. In such states all components of an individual's accessing are likely to cause the person to look down as if at their feet, or belly button.

The technique is firstly to separate all the components back into their *representational systems* and to relocate them into their most common locations (see *eye accessing cues*).

Secondly look up to the right (visual constructed) and create a desired attitude, a goal belief. Adjust the *submodalities* of the belief to make the belief compelling. *Anchor* this state.

Thirdly, move all the representations up into a central location as if the person is looking at the centre of their forehead. As you do so, *linking* them to the constructed outcome or goal, trigger the anchor for the desired outcome to help facilitate this process.

FAMILY THERAPY
A model of therapy which conceptualises the whole family rather than an individual member as the unit of treatment. In

some forms it seeks to interrupt unhelpful patterns of behaviour between family members. It shares many features of NLP as it is *epistemological* in its application.
[See *Bateson, Gregory* and *Satir, Virginia*]

FILTERS
Bandler and ***Grinder*** [7] have described three types of filters or constraints through which our ***model of the world*** is processed. These three filters are neurological, social and individual. The neurological constraints filter our experiences through our sensory organs in building our model. The primary example of social constraint is language which filters the way we think of our world, the way we perceive it, the way we talk about it. Individual constraints operate through both the neurological and the social constraints, and are the sum total of a person's life experiences.
[See *Perceptual Filters*, *Perceptual Position*, *Triple Description*]

FINGER POINTERS
Also referred to simply as "pointers" and sometimes described as a "precision model", these form a useful mnemonic device for dealing with ***meta model*** patterns, and involve the use of the fingers of each hand. One hand represents the recognition of the linguistic patterns which need expanding into their ***deep structure***, the other hand represents the meta model responses to those patterns.

The fingers of the "recognition hand" comprise the generalisations ("all", "never", "every"), the non-specific verbs, the non-specific nouns, the rules ("should", "ought", "must", "can't"), and the comparisons ("too much", "too many", "too little", "too few").

The fingers of the "response hand" provide the questions which enable us to identify and deal with the meta model pattern in a totally effective way. The responses which correspond to the recognition hand patterns are, in the case of generalisations, to raise the corresponding finger and repeat the offending word as a question ("all?", "never?"). Verbs and nouns are questioned as: "how specifically? and "who specifically?". Rules are asked the question: "what would happen if. . . ?" Comparisons are asked: "compared to what?".

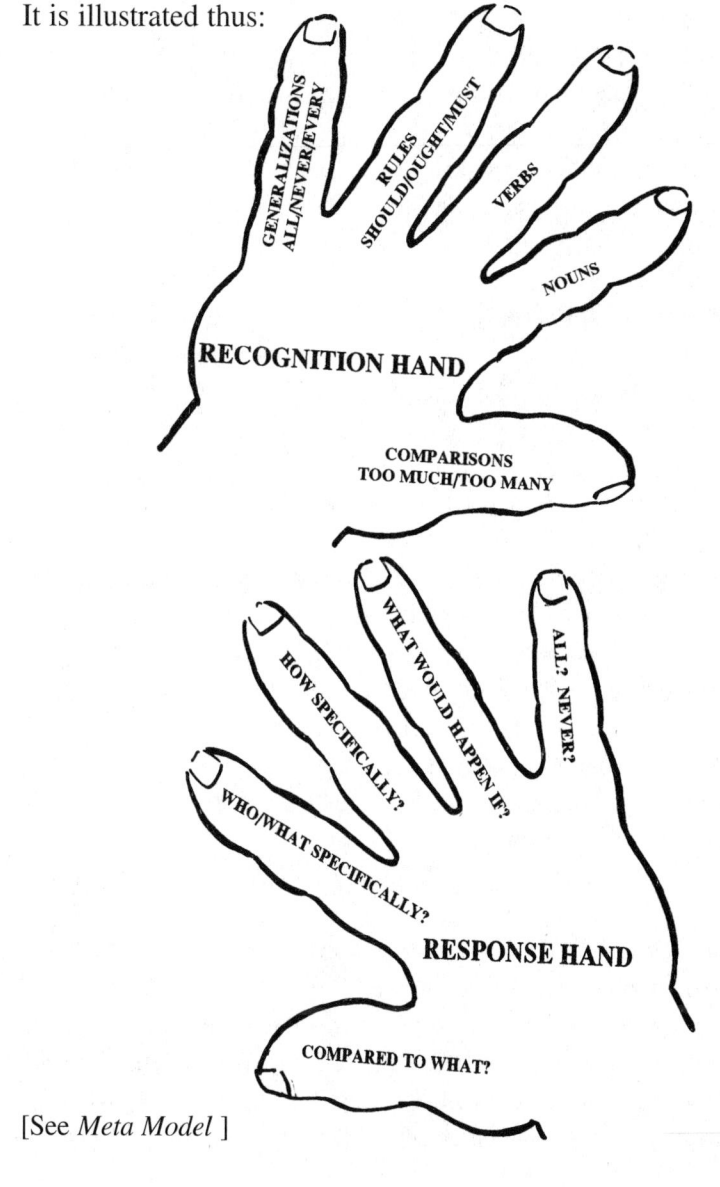

It is illustrated thus:

RECOGNITION HAND
- GENERALIZATIONS ALL/NEVER/EVERY
- RULES SHOULD/OUGHT/MUST
- VERBS
- NOUNS
- COMPARISONS TOO MUCH/TOO MANY

RESPONSE HAND
- WHO/WHAT SPECIFICALLY?
- HOW SPECIFICALLY?
- WHAT WOULD HAPPEN IF?
- ALL? NEVER?
- COMPARED TO WHAT?

[See *Meta Model*]

FIRE
A triggered response. When an *anchor* has been set up it is said to be triggered if the anchor has been set up inadvertently and unconsciously. However, where anchors have been deliberately set up, then these may be consciously triggered or fired either by others, or the persons concerned themselves.

FIRST ATTENTION
A term borrowed from Carlos Castaneda's book *The Fire From Within*.[9] What we usually call consciousness, the dynamic process of picking out what parts of the world are to be sampled in awareness.
[See *New Code NLP*]

FIRST POSITION
The first of at least three *perceptual positions*. Our own view of the world: the one in which we perceive the world from our own vantage point.
[See *Triple Description, Logical Levels, Turtles*]

FLEXIBILITY
In the NLP context, flexibility means having multiple choices on which to act. In Frogs into Princes *Bandler* and *Grinder* specify a meta-rule ingredient as "If what you are doing is not working, change it. Do something else." The more choices we have, the greater our flexibility.

They also suggest that, lacking choice, we are merely robots; given one alternative creates a dilemma; three choices and we have flexibility.
[See Meta-Model]

FOURTH POSITION
Defined by Peter Wrycza[10] as visceral self knowledge of what is happening in a relationship. He says that in fourth position we are not observing but sensing through direct identification what is happening among the couples and groups of which we are a part.

It is the space between you and others in a relationship.
[See *Triple description, Turtles*]

FOUR-TUPLE (4-TUPLE)
At any one moment in time our perceptions and our experiences are determined by our senses: hearing, seeing, feeling, tasting, and smelling. In NLP the last two are usually lumped together and, in the coding system habitually adopted by NLP, the senses are often given the acronym VAKOG, where V=Visual, A=Auditory, K=Kinaesthetic, and OG taken together as Olfactory/Gustatory. These "four" senses form a 4-tuple when applied to any particular moment of experience. Some NLP practitioners, however, regard the 4-tuple instead as referring to only the VAK (OG being regarded as part of K) with the addition of L for Language.
[See also: *R-Operator, TOTE*]

FRAME/FRAMING
The structure within which we place perceptions and events in order to give them meaning; the way in which we put them into different contexts.
[See *"As-if" Frame, Outcomes*]

FUTURE PACING
Stated in its simplest terms it enables us to experience a situation in advance. Put in more complex fashion, it allows us mentally to examine an ***outcome*** by projecting a situation into the future, in order to explore what behaviour pattern might be induced. Observation of someone's ***sensory feedback*** provides clues to the comfort or otherwise of how they will be in the proposed situation. The technique of future pacing can be used both to change or improve an existing behaviour pattern, or to produce an entirely new type of behaviour.

We can engage in several mental exercises in order to review the possibilities available from future pacing. Various behavioural options can be mentally created, examined, reviewed, and considered.

Past behaviour patterns can be recalled, relived and reviewed; after the subject has imagined how such behaviour might have been modified, it can then be mentally achieved, put into a changed context, considered in the new light, and then checked for acceptability.

Mentally rehearsing new behaviour patterns is a powerful and extremely effective tool for personal development, but, as our cartoon suggests, it may be capricious when associated with the following topic - **generalisation**.

GENERALISATION

The process whereby we perceive general experiences on the basis of limited specific experiences. **Bandler** and **Grinder**[7] give the example of a child touching a hot stove and generalising either that "all stoves are hot", or that "hot stoves should not be touched".

Such a generalisation may be a useful learning process, but, as Bandler and Grinder put it, *"to generalise this experience to a perception that stoves are dangerous and, therefore, to refuse to be in the same room with one, is to limit unnecessarily our movement in the world."* Other generalisations may be not only less useful, but emphatically limiting. In NLP it is important to avoid forming judgements on the basis of one type of *accessing cue*, but these should be cross-referenced against other observable behaviour and experience.

Generalisation is one of the three mechanisms common to all model-building activities. The others are *deletion* and *distortion*. These are known as the *"universal human modelling processes"*[7].

"A person who has at some time in his life been rejected makes the generalisation that he's not worth caring for. As his model has this generalisation, he either deletes caring messages or he reinterprets [distorts] these messages as insincere... This description is an example of the classical positive feedback loop: the self-fulfilling prophecy... A person's generalisations or expectations filter out and distort his experience to make it consistent with those expectations." [7]

To a great extent we are able to learn rapidly by the process of generalisation. Generalising from past experiences enables us to save time and energy learning new behaviours, and we do not have to relearn a concept or behaviour every time we are faced with a variation of the original.

We are alerted to generalisations by the use of words such as *all*, *every*, *everyone*, and *always*; but generalisations are

less easy to spot when these words are omitted though implied. The effective way to deal with a generalisation is to repeat the key word as a question, or to request specific information. For example: "Why blame me! Everyone does it." Response: "Everyone?" or "Who specifically?"
[See *Meta Model*]

GESTALT THERAPY
A form of psychotherapy rooted in the here and now of spontaneous experience. It sees communication as a two way negotiation between an organism and its environment. The psychological space between the organism and environment where this negotiation takes place is called the contact boundary. When this negotiation results in the dominance of the environment over the individual, or the individual's manipulation of their environment, an interruption to contact is said to have taken place. Gestalt therapy is concerned with 'dissolving' these interruptions so that a natural, healthy, balanced and ecological relationship is restored.
[See *Perls, Frederick S.*]

GESTURES
The use of bodily movement, posture and looks which may indicate the particular sensory system being activated. Tilting the head, for example, may indicate an **internal auditory dialogue**, rubbing the eyes may indicate a failure to understand what is being said (i.e. a failure to "see").

GRINDER, JOHN
Assistant Professor of Linguistics at the University of California, Santa Cruz, in the early seventies, whose collaboration with **Richard Bandler** was the catalyst for NLP.
[Works include: *Frogs Into Princes, Reframing* and *Transformations* (with Richard Bandler); *The Structure of Magic*, Vols.1 and 2 (with Richard Bandler); *Patterns of the Hypnotic Techniques of Milton H Erickson,* Vols.1 and 2

(with Richard Bandler); *Precision, High Quality Information Processing for Business* (with Michael McMaster), *Turtles all the Way Down* (With Judith DeLozier) and *Leaves Before the Wind* (with Charlotte Bretto)

GUSTATORY
Connected with the sense of taste. Gustatory and *olfactory* are often treated for simplicity as part of the *kinaesthetic* sense in NLP *representational systems*.

HIERARCHY
A hierarchy is a body of persons or things arranged one above another according to rank or priority.

HIERARCHY OF CRITERIA
Our *criteria* differ from our *values*, being less universal and more specific; they determine what motivates us and why we do certain things. Since some criteria are more important to us than others it is useful, in dealing with an issue, to place our criteria in order of priority in order to establish the criterion which it is most important for us to satisfy.

For example, in deciding to move house, we may consider whether the location is more important than the people we will (a) leave behind us and (b) find as our new neighbours. If we consider the new location to be more desirable, we might then wish to consider whether it is more important to us than, say, the extra distance we shall have to travel to work.

HIERARCHY OF VALUES
We all have inter-connected *belief systems* and *values*, which are acquired from family, friends, teachers and experience. Often the values are unconscious; we make choices, take decisions and are motivated sometimes without knowing quite why we do so.

In as much as these values differ from those of other individuals, we give them different orders of importance or priority. Our hierarchy of values is the arrangement of priority we give to them, and will differ from the hierarchy of values of others. One of the useful skills in negotiation is to determine the hierarchy of values of the other party, in order to address the value with the highest order of priority.

HUMAN ACTIVITY SYSTEM

A special type of *system* which relies on the quality of human interaction in order to function. Businesses, families and NLP training programmes are all examples of human activity systems.

Some might assert that since human beings are a part of the natural world, then a human activity system is merely a class of *natural system*. Such an argument ignores the fact that humans, whilst sharing the attribute of having emergent properties with natural systems, also have a metacognative ability. That is to say they are able to think about how they think.

In fairy stories frogs are anthropomorphised to think like humans. In the natural world a frog shares the ability to be conceptualised as a whole entity; in the same way as a prince. However, only the prince will be able to imagine what it may be like to be a frog, or a beggar, and to *model* each if he wishes to do so.

The ability to think in this way causes a human being to be less predictable than a natural system. For example, faced with the sudden movement of a predator the frog will have limited options available to him; he is likely to jump for cover. A human being however, may choose to take cover, to stand and fight, to mimic the assailant in attempt to use humour to defuse the situation, or s/he may choose to pray for lasting peace and happiness in an unseen realm above.

As human beings are a component of human activity systems, then these need to be treated according to a different set of rules than those appertaining to mechanical, or natural systems.

[see *System Theory*]

IDENTIFYING OUTCOMES
Becoming aware of what resources are needed to achieve a desired result. In formulating outcomes it is important that they should be positive in content, attainable, and environmentally appropriate. Asking the right questions helps us to identify our outcomes. Thus "What do I want?", "How will I know if I've got it?", "What will I be doing/seeing/hearing/feeling when I have reached my outcome?". [See *Outcomes* for a more detailed description]

IDENTITY
My image of myself; my conception of my quality and my worth.

INCONGRUENCE
That situation wherein uncertainty as to needs and desired **outcomes** lead to discord in behaviour patterns and sensory systems.

In such a situation we communicate a set of messages through our **output channels**, e.g. breathing, posture, body language, tonality, language, tempo, gestures which are incongruent, i.e. which do not match and are not compatible.

Gregory Bateson says, *"What is known to occur at the animal level is the simultaneous presentation of contradictory signals - postures which mention both aggression and flight, and the like. These ambiguities are, however, quite different from the phenomenon familiar among humans where the friendliness of a man's words may be contradicted by the tension or aggressiveness of his voice or posture. The man is engaging in a sort of deceit, an altogether more complex achievement."*[4]

Incongruency can be attributed to a lack of communication between our sub-personalities or ***parts***. Our internal conflicts, those times when we cannot make up our minds, reflect differences between one part of our personality and another. These conflicting messages are frequently the result of parental messages: we may have introjected parental behaviour patterns along with parental injunctions and "drivers". When one of these patterns conflicts with another we experience incongruency.

Incongruency is a way by which the process of achieving our desired *outcomes* becomes frustrated. It is a guarantee that we shall fail in any attempt to achieve our goals. Conflicting messages will be received by those with whom we wish to communicate, creating an impression of dishonesty or weakness.
[See *Congruence, Introjection, Paramessages, Parts Negotiation*]

INPUT CHANNELS
The brain receives, absorbs, sorts, stores and uses information

from external or internal sources via the five senses of sight, hearing, feeling, taste and smell. These are sometimes referred to as input channels.
[See *TOTE* and *New Code NLP*]

INSTALLATION
The process of facilitating the acquisition of a new strategy of behaviour. A new *strategy* may be installed through some combination of *anchoring*, *accessing cues*, *metaphors*, and *future pacing*.
[See: *Failure into Feedback*]

INTEGRATING LINKS
Anchoring a negative and a positive state simultaneously, which serves to increase the response options of the individual in any given situation.
[See *Links*. Also known as *Collapsing Anchors*]

INTENTION
The purpose of *behaviour*, or its desired *outcome*. It is important for me to distinguish between what I am doing (my behaviour), and what I am hoping to achieve by my behaviour (my intention). Identifying intention is very important in *reframing*, which is involved with changing unwanted behaviour.
[See *Logical Levels*]

INTERNAL AUDITORY DIALOGUE
An inner voice located in the auditory system, whereby we talk things over with ourselves internally, rehearsing arguments, running through responses, etc.
[See *Eye Accessing Cues*]

INTERNAL REPRESENTATIONS
The arrangement of information we create and store in our minds in the form of pictures, sounds, feeling, smells and tastes.

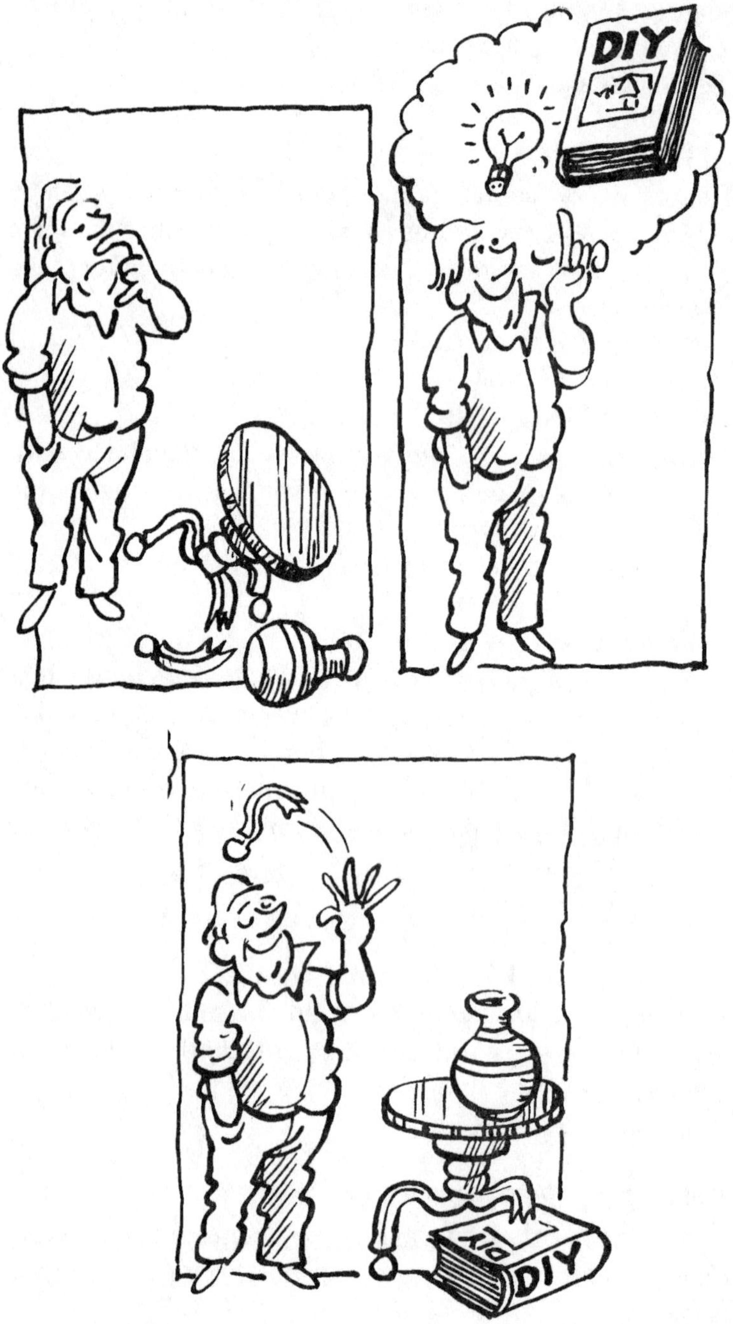
DIY
DIY

We recall past experiences or places by referring to our internal representations. We also imagine future events in the same way.

Our internal representation of an event becomes totally personalised by being passed through our filtering system. It will not necessarily be the same as the representation of another viewer who has different values, attitudes and personal beliefs.

We can change the things we represent or how we represent them by using the key *submodalities* that trigger responses within us. Thus we can brighten a mental picture of a future event and make it more appealing; or, if our representational system is predominantly auditory or kinaesthetic, we can imagine the future event sounding happier, or feeling more cosy. Similarly with past events. By brightening or darkening our memory-picture we can adjust our response to the past situation.

"The key to producing the results you desire . . . is to represent things to yourself in a way that puts you in such a resourceful state that you're empowered to take the types and qualities of actions that create your desired outcomes . . .

" If we represent to ourselves that things aren't going to work, they won't. If we form a representation that things will work, then we create the internal resources we need to produce the state that will support us in producing positive results."[3]

IN TIME
To be *associated* in an experience as if it is happening. Said to be more common in traditional cultures than western ones. [See also: *Through Time*]

INTROJECTION
The assimilation into our unconscious of a behaviour pattern or attitude adopted from another person. This pattern is likely to behave in a semiautonomous way as a *part* which may be

corrupting our natural behaviour patterns.
[See *Perls, Frederick S*]

INTUITION
The ability to arrive at consistent judgements without conscious awareness of how those judgements are made. In NLP it has great value in its use to judge **well-formedness** in sentence structure by native speakers of the language being used.
   "*If you want to have the same intuitions as somebody like Erickson or Satir or Perls, you need to go through a training period to learn to have similar intuitions . . .*"[1] While this is not the only way to enjoy such intuitions, it certainly demonstrates a novel approach to the subject whereby the whole is studied before the parts are assembled, turning on its head the traditional method of study.
[See *Learning Theory, Unconscious Mind*]

K
A symbol representing kinaesthetic
[See *TOTE Notation*]

KINAESTHETIC
That **sensory system** which pertains to body sensation; also includes internal feelings (constructed or remembered) and external feelings which are experienced. **Representational systems** in an NLP context sometimes include the senses of taste and smell in the kinaesthetic sense.
[See *Four Tuple*]

LANGUAGE
"*Language is apparently a sword which cuts both ways. With its help man can conquer the unknown; with it he can grievously wound himself.*"[11]
   Language is the name we give to the vehicle we use for communicating ideas. We encode perceptual phenomena into awareness which is manipulated by the mind in order to

make sense out of experience. Features of this awareness are objectified and associated with sounds. When these sounds are uttered and become the recognised sounds for the objectified phenomena they are referred to as words. These words even when linked are not yet a language. Monosyllabic or simple structures are possible, but these are a simple code. A language must be able to convey complex concepts about objects, actions, attributes, past, present and future. Anyone who has watched a child develop from 18 months to 8 years will fully understand this description.

Language develops as a result of the use of words over the course of one or two generations giving rise to a rich representation of experience. This includes a sense of past, present and future and an accepted grammatical syntax.

Language is, capable of both enhancing and limiting our perception of the world; for example, *"Eskimos have some seventy different words for snow"*[2]; and much language, particularly of the more primitive kind, is not primarily concerned with ideas at all.

For language adequately to communicate concepts, it must be able to transmit the **deep structure** of a message. Since the word is not the experience, a language must be able (a) to interpret an idea properly; (b) to form a legitimate internal representation of that idea; and (c) to convey an adequately accurate internal representation of that idea to the other person. Everyday language is economical in its use of words and so the deep structure is implied via a process of rules which are biologically and culturally determined. Everyday language is the **surface structure** of a communication. That is to say that it is the **deep structure** filtered via biological constraints and social rules into the simplest form capable of containing meaning.

The problem in communicating by language arises from the fact that we each have our own, unique representation of reality, i.e. we do not all share the same **model of the world**. It is easy for us to accept a failure to communicate when speaking to (or listening to) someone in another language with which we/they are unfamiliar. It is less easy to appreciate, when we are both using the same language, that we may be suffering a similar failure to communicate, because we are interpreting words in a different way, or because we are using different **representational systems**.

"There's an illusion that people understand each other when they repeat the same words. But since those words internally access different experience - which they must - then there's always going to be a difference in meaning.

"There's a slippage between the word and the experience,

and there's also a slippage between my corresponding experience for a word and your corresponding experience for the same word. I think it's extremely useful for you to behave so that your clients.....have the illusion that you understand what they are saying verbally. I caution you against accepting the illusion for yourself."[2]
[See also *Ambiguity, Communication, Logical Semantic Relations, Perceptual Filters, Semantics, Syntax*]

LATERAL EYE MOVEMENTS
[See *Eye Accessing Cues*]

LEADING
Part of a technique known as ***pacing*** and leadin*g*. Pacing has the objective of establishing ***rapport*** with another person. Leading, involves adopting subtle behaviour changes as a way of determining whether rapport has been successfully established, in which event the other person will also alter their behaviour and follow our lead.

In cases where good rapport has been established a person may be led into a different understanding or physiological state as an aid to communication or change.

This is one of the areas where critics have laid the charge of manipulation at NLP [See ***Manipulation***]. Since some degree of rapport is an essential ingredient to any therapeutic technique, the same charge could, perhaps, be levelled at any therapeutic endeavour.

LEARNING, FOUR STAGES OF
In learning, we proceed from (1) unconscious incompetence to (2) conscious incompetence, then through (3) conscious competence to (4) unconscious competence.

Thus we begin at a level where we are unaware of our incompetence (e.g. a child unable to walk) to a level where our incompetence enters our consciousness (the child recognises that others around it are walking, but is as yet unable to emulate them). Conscious competence arrives with the child's first faltering steps and only becomes unconscious competence when it finally walks without having to concentrate on the act of walking.

The same four stages apply to the learning of any skill. A patterned response, which has been stabilised at the level of unconscious competence is known as an *engram*. These engrams are beneficial if they involve automatic activities which are useful, but also comprise activities which are automatic and pernicious, such as addictive behaviour.

NLP can teach us how to reinforce those patterns which we like, and how to change the harmful or unsatisfactory patterns by changing our mental state.
[See *State, State of Excellence*]

LEARNING, SIMPLE AND COMPLEX
Simple learning is making a habit of a simple response. It is also known as stimulus-response. Learning our name, responding to it when it is called, is an example of habit learning. Adding numbers at a simple level, i.e. without

trying to understand what they may represent at a higher level, is another instance of simple learning. Complex learning, also known as cognitive memory learning, involves the "how", "what" and "why" of our learning, associating the learning with intellectual or emotional response.

[See *Anchoring, Learning Four Stages Of*]

LIFE PATTERNS

Responses to stimuli which have occurred throughout an individual's life. Blaming and complaining (particularly when we feel guilty), putting ourselves down, frequent apologising or acting apologetically (again often having a guilt motivation), all these are negative life patterns. NLP has specific exercises to enable us to deal with negative patterns in ourselves and also in others. NLP also has powerful exercises to determine a positive *outcome* in order to revise negative responses on a long-term basis.

[See *Change History, Reframing, Re-Imprinting*]

LEVELS OF CHANGE

[See: *Logical Levels, Unified Field Theory*]

LINKAGE

[See Linking]

LINKING

Linking occurs when a stimulus creates a predictable pattern of behaviour.

(a) Negative Linking. A negative response to a particular stimulus might result in, say, anxiety.

(b) Positive Linking. A positive response to a particular stimulus could result in an optimistic approach to any challenge.

[See *Anchoring, Chaining Anchors*]

LOGICAL LEVELS

An internal hierarchy or organisation in which each level is progressively more psychologically encompassing and impactful. In order of importance (from high to low) these levels include (1) identity, (2) beliefs and values, (3) capabilities, (4) behaviour, and (5) environment. Much of the theory of Logical Levels in NLP derives from the pioneering work of **Gregory Bateson** as developed by **Robert Dilts**.

As an example:
(1) Identity. "I am a smoker and will always be a smoker."
(2) Belief . "I have to smoke in order to relax."
(3) Capability. "I can't control my smoking."
(4) Specific Behaviour. "I smoked too much last night."
(5) Environment. "When I'm alone I find I smoke a lot."

Here's an illustration of Logical Levels provided by Michael Mallows [*Groupvine 1992*]:

Employee: "It's not my fault (BELIEF) I'm doing badly (CAPABILITY); the neon lighting affected my eyes (ENVIRONMENT) and I couldn't concentrate (BEHAVIOUR)."

Supervisor: "I don't think (BELIEF) that you made the necessary phone calls (BEHAVIOUR)."

Employee: "I've not really had sufficient training for this job." (CAPABILITY)

Supervisor: "Well, you're a rotten worker! (IDENTITY) But I owe you a favour (VALUES)."

Employee: "Well, I'll leave (BEHAVIOUR). I don't want to stay where I'm not wanted (BELIEFS/VALUES). Anyway, I'm too good for this job (IDENTITY)."

In this example, the supervisor may be addressing one logical level, e.g. *behaviour*, not realising that the employee's problem, and the supervisor's own longer term solution, may need to be addressed on a different logical level, e.g. *identity*. [See also *Spirit, Triple Description*]

LOGICAL SEMANTIC RELATIONS
In linguistics these are the relations reflected between sentences or parts of sentences such as:
(a) *ambiguity*, or conveying two or more possible meanings;
(b) *completeness*, or having no ambiguity;
(c) *synonymy*, i.e. two sentences conveying the same meaning;
(d) *referential indices*, or identifying whether a word or phrase applies to a specific or a general object;
(e) *presuppositions*, namely beliefs which are an extension of a statement made in a sentence.

MAGIC
When **Bandler** and **Grinder** first set out on the course of studies that was later to become the basis for NLP they sought to understand the patterns common to three highly successful therapists. These therapists they referred to as Wizards; and what they had in common, Bandler and Grinder referred to as magic.

Of the many influences cited in the live workshops of NLP to provide a metaphor, or to develop an idea, is the writing of Carlos Castaneda. This work describes the training and initiation of an individual following a contemporary shaman's path. The Shaman's teacher is called Don Juan. Castaneda's work was frequently quoted in therapeutic circles during the 1970's and so it is not remarkable to find him mentioned in the final paragraphs of *Frogs into Princes 1979*. He appears again in *Reframing 1981*, and by 1987 **John Grinder** and **Judith DeLozier** quote him no less than ten times in the transcript of their five day workshop, *Turtles all the Way Down*.

But it is not Castaneda's Don Juan who makes the first entry into the magical world of Bandler and Grinder, for veiled within a charming quotation in the preface to *The Structure of Magic* Vol. 1, we find Maurice Conchis, the sinister sorcerer from John Fowles's novel *The Magus*:

Father is it true that you are not a real king, but only a magician?"

The king smiled and rolled back his sleeves.
"Yes my son, I'm only a magician."
"Then the man on the other shore was God."
"The man on the other shore was another magician."
"I must know the truth, the truth beyond magic"
"There is no truth beyond magic," said the king[2].
[See *First Attention, New Code NLP, Second Attention*]

MANIPULATION
Achieving my own *outcome* at the expense of someone else. Achieving my own outcome while respecting the outcome of the other party is not manipulative but influencing. NLP has been described by some critics as manipulative. However, NLP is in many ways like a language, it has a dual nature. When examined on paper it is a noun, but when it is operating in the world it is a process, (or a verb). Through NLP both parties communicate recursively. Speech is a process. I can use speech to manipulate; is it then speech which is manipulative, or am I being manipulative? I can also use speech to influence for good. Is it then speech which is good? Or am I doing good?

Within the *unified field theory* manipulation is a *non sequitur*. However, knowledge derived from NLP may be abstracted from this context and distorted by manipulative people.
[See *Dovetailing Outcomes, Negotiation*]

MAP OF REALITY
[See *Model of the World*]

MAPPING
A process whereby we may determine a person's preferred *representational system* in use at any one time; their *eye accessing patterns*; whether they are oriented to the past present or future; if they are *associated* or *dissociated* and the *logical level* at which they are operating.

MATCHING

Subtly adopting the behaviour patterns of another person in order to achieve or improve *rapport* by imitating their tone of voice, style of speech, facial expressions, or matching their breathing pattern or posture. This is not done in an exaggerated or obvious manner if the aim is to improve rapport. The opposite technique is also a useful skill: deliberately mis-matching in order to break rapport, perhaps in order to end an encounter or interrupt the pattern when negotiating.
[See *Cross Over Matching, Mismatching*]

MEMORY

Our short-term memory will apparently hold no more than nine bits of information efficiently and effectively at any one time. George Miller [*The Magical Number Seven, Plus*

or Minus Two (1956)] demonstrated that the human mind can deal with no more than seven bits of information, plus or minus two; (depending on personal constraints), consciously and comfortably. Things like a new telephone number, or the name of someone you have just met, can be retained in short-term memory, but only by conscious effort and repetition can such material be retained indefinitely in short-term memory.

Furthermore, simplicity is an aid to retention; the more easily something is understood, the more easily it is retained in memory; the less easily it is understood, the sooner we forget it.

There is also a real difference between short-term and long-term memory. Short-term memory is immediate and direct, whereas time and effort is needed to put new material into long-term memory.

Leo Tolstoy [*The History of Yesterday*, 1851] wrote: *"In all our memories the middle disappears, and only the first and last impression, especially the last one, remains."* We call this the serial position effect. In free recall situations, the last material presented to a learner is best recalled, and the early material is recalled better than what appeared in the middle.
[See *Miller, George*]

MENTAL REHEARSAL
Using one's imagination to prepare for and practice some future event. It can be used to generate new behaviour, and can be very effective in improving one's actual performance in the event.

In **gestalt therapy** it is rehearsing a situation in such a way as to limit spontaneity, or to create a negative outcome.
[See *Future Pacing, Perls, Frederick S.*]

MENTAL SYNTAX
The way we organise our thoughts. Just as grammatical syntax is concerned with the arrangement of words, and their

connection and relationship with the structure of sentences, so mental syntax is concerned with the arrangement of our thoughts and their connection and relationship with our brains and nervous systems.
[See *Syntax*]

META
Linguistically *meta*, deriving from the Greek (with, or in common with), when prefixed to the name of a science, serves to designate a higher science of the same nature, but dealing with ulterior problems. ***Epistemology*** is a meta science.
[See *Second Order Cybernetics*]

METACOGNITION
Corresponding to the level of unconscious competence in the ***four stages of learning***, but knowing what one knows: being able to bring a task to the conscious level and explain it.
[See Uptime]

META MODEL
The meta model is a systematic aid to communication based on the rules of ***transformational grammar***. It reunites language and experience. Just as the word meta is defined as a linguistic prefix which deals with the concealed issues of a particular science, so the meta-model deals with the hidden uses of language in order to interpret language, make it more precise, remove ambiguities and ensure that it corresponds to the ***sensory experience*** and ***deep structure*** from which it sprang. To achieve this the meta model employs a series of questions designed to overcome the problems of ***deletion***, ***distortion*** and ***generalisation*** which customarily afflict our language.

Thus, in order to make subjects face up to the specific and basic nature of their statements, the meta model asks such questions as: What precisely...? Who specifically...? Where precisely...? How specifically...? Compared with what...? Who is saying that? How is that happening? What is stopping you from...? Has there ever been a time when...? What would happen if...? These questions provide immediate access to appropriate information.

The questions, the reasons why they are asked, the way in which they all deal with meta model violations, are treated separately under the following headings: *Cause and Effect, Comparisons, Complex Equivalence, Generalisations, Modal Operators of Necessity, Modal Operators of Possibility, Nominalizations, Presuppositions, Unspecified Nouns, Unspecified Verbs, Universal Quantifiers.*

Rudyard Kipling may have anticipated the meta model when he wrote,

> I had six honest serving men
> They taught me all I knew:
> Their names were Where and What and When
> And Why and How and Who.

Adding the word "specifically" would have destroyed his metre-model.

"The meta-model is really simplistic, but it's still the foundation of everything we do... The difference between the people who do the things we teach well and those that don't, are people who have control over the meta-model."[2]

A useful mnemonic device for dealing with meta model patterns involves the use of the fingers of each hand. One hand represents the recognition of the meta model patterns, the other hand represents the responses to those patterns.
[*A description and an illustration of this mnemonic is given under* **Finger Pointers**   See also the *Meta Model example* on page 81]

METAPHORS

Stories, parables, anecdotes or similes, folk tales, fairy tales and myths, simple comparisons; all are metaphors in the context of NLP. And all of them, when properly constructed, and creatively presented, are able to provide non-threatening

META MODEL

RECOGNITION	RESPONSE
Simple deletion "I am worried"	"Worried about what, specifically?"
Comparative deletion "There is more than there should be"	"How much less should there be?"
Unspecified referential index "Children will not work"	"Which children specifically?"
Unspecified verbs "I have problems with maths"	"What are the problems that you have with maths, specifically?"
Nominalizations "The relationship ended"	"Who was relating to whom, about what, and in what way?"
Modal operator of necessity "I must learn this material"	"What will happen if you do?" "What will happen if you don't?"
Modal operator of possibility "I can't learn this material"	"What stops you?"
Presuppositions "If he suffered as I do, then he wouldn't be able to act as he does"	"How do you know he doesn't suffer in the same way as you?" "How is he acting?"
Universal quantifiers "She always wants her own way"	"Always?" "Can you think of a time when she didn't?"
Cause-effect "Her lack of concentration annoys me"	"What specifically about her lack of concentration annoys you?" "How does it annoy you?"
Mind reading "She thinks that she's the cat's whiskers"	"How do you know she has that opinion of herself?"
Complex equivalence "He only chooses soft drinks. He is a recovering alcoholic"	"How specifically does choosing to drink soft drinks mean that he's an alcoholic?"
Lost performatives "It's good to put other people's needs before your own"	"According to whom is this good?" "How specifically is this good?"

experiences which, used effectively, may result in profound and long-term behavioural change.

Metaphors work on both the conscious and unconscious mental levels. A simple metaphor, i.e. a simple comparison, will induce an immediate conscious response and will enable the listener to view something in a new way; complex metaphors may disguise their real intent, but are able to stimulate some comprehension of their true meaning, albeit unconsciously.

Because of this ability to appeal to the unconscious mind, **Milton Erickson** used metaphors extensively in his hypnotherapy sessions.

Businessmen - "captains of industry" - have long recognised the benefits of metaphor. Henry Ford was a master of metaphor. *"Business is never so healthy,"* he once said, *"as when, like a chicken, it must do a certain amount of scratching for what it gets."* Which was surely more effective than the more prosaic: *"Go out and hustle!"*
[See *Therapeutic Metaphor*]

META PROGRAMME
Meta Programmes are the deepest level of basic programmes that filter our perception.[12]
There are nine components to the meta programme:
1. Toward the Positive vs. Away from the Negative
2. Match (seek out sameness) vs. Mismatch (seek out differences)
3. Past (Remembered); Present (External); Future (Constructed)
4. Associated (In Time) vs. Dissociated (Through Time)
5. Toward External Behaviour vs. Internal Response
6. Referring to Self? Other? Context? or Spirit? (Corresponding to **First, Second, Third** and **Fourth Positions**)
7. Sorting by: Who? What? Where? When? or How? (Person, Information, Place, Time and Behaviour)
8. Chunking: Up (specific to general); Down (general to

specific) or Lateral (through analogy).
9. Value orientation toward: Power, Affiliation or Achievement.

Individual *parts* of an individual or organisation may operate out of different meta programmes. They provide a useful tool in the contexts of psychotherapy and organisational consulting.

MILLER, GEORGE
Author of a paper entitled *The Magical Number Seven, Plus or Minus Two*[13] which, together with the publication of *Plans and Structure of the Brain*[14] (with Galanter and Pribram), was to have a significant impact on NLP. It was from Miller that the early developers of NLP borrowed the concept of the ***TOTE***.

MILTON MODEL
A model of ***Milton H. Erickson's*** use of language in such a way as to induce a trance state, which is then employed to access the unconscious resources of the personality, while the conscious mind is being distracted. The language is used in a deliberately vague manner in contrast to the precision of the ***meta-model***.

The Milton model chunks up; the meta model chunks down.
[See *Chunking*]

MIND
One of the two royal roads to understanding ***states***. The other being ***physiology***. The content of our personal history as we have modelled the perceptions received via the five senses. Also, the words we say to ourselves, about ourselves and our perceptions.

MIND READING
The belief that a person can know the thoughts or feelings of another person without direct evidence, and without

checking them out. When we mind read, it usually represents projection of our own thoughts or feelings and can lead to much misunderstanding and argument. A typical **meta model** challenge would be "I wonder quite how you know. . .?" or "What leads you to think. . .?" or "Would you mind telling me. . ."

[See *Presuppositions*]

MINIMAL CUES

The slight shifts or variation in physiology which are often indicative of subtle messages that ordinarily might be unobserved on the conscious level. Minute muscle changes, breathing changes, skin colour changes, all may be subtle indications of emotional state. Rounded shoulders and curved spine, for example, might indicate that a person is "going inside" to process information; alternatively a straightening of the spine and tensing of the shoulders may indicate that a person is processing information visually.

[See *Calibration, Sensory Acuity*]

[See MISMATCHING]

MIRRORING
The technique of matching the behaviour patterns of another person in order to establish *rapport*, i.e. subtly copying their gestures, facial expressions, etc. as though seen in a mirror.
[See *Matching*]

MISMATCHING
Deliberately breaking *rapport* by the use of contradictory behaviour patterns, for the purpose of redirecting or severing communication.
[See *Matching*]

MODAL OPERATOR
Modal operator is a linguistic term used to define the boundaries of our conduct and distinguished by such words as "should, "must", "can't" and "ought". Modal operators circumscribe and limit our *model of the world*. Modal operators restrict our awareness of the choices open to us, and any attempt to extend our awareness beyond the established boundaries is to place the result outside our control, and to invite disaster.

One way of expanding my model of the world and giving me a greater range of choice of thoughts and feelings is, therefore, to remove the boundaries, allowing me to develop other patterns of behaviour.

This is done by asking questions which will offer new options and fresh choices. Statement: "You must complete that work by Friday." Question: "What would happen if I didn't?" Statement: "You shouldn't settle for second best." Question: "What would happen if I did?"
[See *Meta Model and the Meta Model Example*]

MODAL OPERATOR OF NECESSITY
The term used to describe those linguistic principles which are based on obligation, or imperatives, recognisable by statements containing such words as "ought", "should", "must". The appropriate *meta model* responses are: "What

do you think would happen if you did not. . .?" "What will happen if you do. . .? This method of asking the subject to examine their expectations causes them to become aware of the underlying messages which first prompted the statement.
[See *Meta-Model Example*]

MODAL OPERATOR OF POSSIBILITY
The term used to describe those linguistic principles which are based on potentially counterproductive limitations of choice, and are discernible by the use of such words as "can", "can't" "could". Appropriate *meta model* responses might be: "What might stop you.. . .? "What might happen if you did. . .?" The use of the word "can't" simply demonstrates that a person is limiting their own perception of a situation. ***Fritz Perls*** would get his subject to substitute the word "won't" for "can't", thus acknowledging that an unwillingness to perform a function is not the result of lack of ability or external circumstance.
[See *Reframing, Meta-Model Example*]

MODALITIES
Another term for sensory experiences.
[See *Representational Systems*, see also *Submodalities*]

MODEL
A description of how something works, with the intention of putting it to practical use.

When creating a model, the processes of ***generalisation***, ***deletion*** and ***distortion*** are the three ways in which the model is made to differ from the thing which it models. A model is inevitably, therefore, a generalised, deleted and distorted copy of what it represents. Nevertheless a model enables us to communicate and operate in a much simpler, more understandable, and more recognisable way. The model itself does not need to be understood - although with use and refinement it ultimately becomes more understandable - but used effectively it will provide similar results to the original on which it is based.

An explorer, having successfully circumvented hazards, will construct a plan or map of the route he has taken. That map or plan, followed by someone else, may not disclose any of the hazards, but will enable the user to make the same progress from A to B as did the explorer.

A master chef will prepare an exquisite dish and faithfully record the procedure followed, calling it a recipe. A novice at producing any culinary originality may copy the recipe carefully and (given the same conditions) precisely reproduce the culinary delight.

[See *Generalisation, Deletion, Distortion; the Meta Model Example*]

MODELLING

The ability to identify the sequence and patterns of thought and behaviour that enable an individual to be able to successfully perform a task.

When **Richard Bandler** and **John Grinder** published *The Structure of Magic* in 1975, they had become fascinated by the emergence from the ranks of modern psychotherapy of *"a number of charismatic superstars"*; people who *"seemingly perform the task of clinical psychology with the ease and wonder of a therapeutic magician."*

Among such "magicians" Bandler and Grinder singled out **Fritz Perls** and **Virginia Satir** as possessing this magical quality.

The intention behind their book was not, however, to explore the reasons why such magic existed in a few individuals, but rather to reveal the structures common to each individual studied which, given the right resources, can be duplicated. The process of duplication is what they called modelling.

Modelling as practised by Bandler and Grinder is predicated in direct observation and analysis of speech patterns using the framework of ***transderivational grammar***. This is now called ***sensory modelling***.

More generally modelling is the process of detecting the sequence of internal representations that enable an individual to perform a task, thereby making it much easier and faster to duplicate the task. The process of detection may involve the discovery of the strategy, language, beliefs, and behaviour of the individual.

"What we essentially do is to pay very little attention to what people say they do and a great deal of attention to what they do and then we build ourselves a model of what they do." [2]

"We are not particularly interested in what's "true". The function of modelling is to arrive at descriptions which are useful." [2]

[See also: *Advanced Modelling Strategy, Conceptual Modelling, Milton Model, Sensory Modelling, Self Modelling, Symbolic Modelling*]

MODEL OF REALITY
[See *Model of the World, Sleight of Mouth Patterns*]

MODEL OF THE WORLD
[Also known as ***Map of Reality***, ***Model of Reality***]
The synthesis of one's behaviour, beliefs and perceptions which enables one to operate in a particular way. Each of us creates our own perception or model of the world and thus, to a greater or lesser extent, we each perceive the world differently, and none of us perceives the "real" world, but merely a "model" of reality, yet we tend to operate as if our model of the world is the real world.

I.S.Hayakawa made the following fascinating and significant comments in his *Language in Thought and Action* [15].

"Let us call this world that comes to us through words the verbal world, as opposed to the world we know or are capable of knowing through our experience, which we shall call the extensional world

...*"Now to use the famous metaphor introduced by Alfred Korzybski in his Science and Sanity (1933), this verbal world* ought to stand in relation to the extensional world as a map does to the territory it is supposed to represent. *If a child grows to adulthood with a verbal world in his head which corresponds fairly closely to the extensional world that he finds around him in his widening experience, he is in relatively small danger of being shocked or hurt by what he finds, because his verbal world has told him what, more or less, to expect. He is prepared for life. If, however, he grows up with a false map in his head - that is, with a head crammed with error and superstition - he will constantly be running into trouble, wasting his efforts, and may, if the lack of adjustment is serious, end up in a mental hospital.*

"Some of the follies we commit because of false maps in our heads are so commonplace that we do not even think of them as remarkable. There are those who protect themselves from accidents by carrying a rabbit's foot.

"Some refuse to sleep on the thirteenth floor of hotels - a situation so common that most big hotels. . .skip '13' in numbering their floors. Some plan their lives on the basis of astrological predictions. . . Some hope to make their teeth whiter by changing their brand of toothpaste. All such people are living in verbal worlds that bear little, if any, resemblance to the extensional world.

"Now, no matter how beautiful a map may be, it is useless to a traveller unless it accurately shows the relationship of places to each other, the structure of the territory. If we draw, for example, a big dent in the outline of a lake for, let us say, artistic reasons, the map is worthless. But if we are just drawing maps for fun without paying any attention to the structure of the region, there is nothing in the world to prevent us from putting in all the extra curlicues and twists we want in the lakes, rivers and roads. No harm will be done unless someone tries to plan a trip by such a map.

"Similarly, by means of imaginary or false reports, or by false inferences from good reports, or by mere rhetorical exercises, we can manufacture at will, with language, 'maps' which have no reference to the extensional world. Here again

no harm will be done unless someone makes the mistake of regarding such 'maps' as representing real territories.

"...the cultural heritage of our civilisation that is transmitted to us...has been valued principally because we have believed that it gives us accurate maps of experience. The analogy of verbal worlds to maps is an important one...[however]...there are two ways of getting false maps of the world into our heads: first, by having them given to us; second, by creating them ourselves when we misread the true maps given to us."

MULTIPLE DESCRIPTION
[See *Triple Description*]

NAGUAL

Not strictly NLP: a magician, sorcerer, shaman such as Don Juan of the Carlos Castaneda narrative. May be used to describe altered states of consciousness, such as those encountered when experiencing the universe directly without recourse to the descriptions of language, such as in trance, or dream states. The opposite of the *Tonal*.
[See: *Magic*]

NATURAL SYSTEM

Part of the natural world, (not man-made), which an observer chooses to treat as a whole entity; for example a frog. Natural systems are said to have emergent properties; that is characteristics which are meaningful only when attributed to the whole, not to its parts.

   Natural systems have a greater level of complexity than mechanical systems, such as clocks. The components which make up the mechanical clock in time will show signs of wear. Some clocks will be constructed to withstand the effects of entropy. However, no clock will be able to repair its spring, or balance wheel in a similar way to how a frog, or any higher organism is able to replace cellular tissue due to its continuously balancing relationship with the environment within which it is able to survive. The behaviour of a clock is therefore more predictable than that of a frog.
[See *Cybernetics, Human Activity System, Systems Theory*]

NEGATIVE LINKING
[See *Linking, Anchoring*]

NEGOTIATION

Any communication between two or more parties whose *outcomes* apparently conflict. In planning a negotiation it is useful to predetermine our desired outcome and to decide on the lowest level of compromise, thus entering the negotiation with both best and worst case options available. It should be noted, however, that compromise is a lose-lose situation in the sense that both parties are required to give something up; negotiation is a win-win situation in the sense that, by *dovetailing outcomes*, both parties end up gaining. [See *BATNA, Dovetailing Outcomes, Manipulation*]

NEURO-LINGUISTIC PROGRAMMING (NLP)
In essence NLP is a modelling system which was developed in the early 1970s by people whose background comprised cybernetics, mathematics, and linguistics. **John Grinder** and **Richard Bandler** were both at the University of California, Santa Cruz; the former as an assistant professor of linguistics, the latter a student of psychology and a mathematician. Modelling, in the context of NLP, is the process of discovering exactly and specifically how people produce their precise results, and replicating them.

It is based on the assumption that, since we all share the

same neurology, we can successfully replicate anyone else if we follow their actions and behaviours precisely.

Grinder and Bandler combined their talents in pursuit of models of successful therapeutic systems and took as their ideals **Fritz Perls** the originator of *Gestalt Therapy,* **Virginia Satir**, a very successful innovator in *Family Therapy*, and **Milton H. Erickson**, a renowned hypnotherapist.

In modelling these individuals, they extracted those parts which were most useful and productive, and discarded those parts of the original theories of each of the three which were irrelevant to the development of useful patterns of change and relationships. Their discovery was that three major ingredients needed to be replicated: a person's ***belief system***, their ***mental syntax***, and their ***physiology***.

Bandler and Grinder were aided by **Gregory Bateson** an expert in anthropology and cybernetics, and joined by **Judith DeLozier** and Leslie Cameron-Bandler.

Neuro Linguistic Programming is so named because it is based on the study of how behaviour stems from neurological processes, how language is used in communication, and how we program our behaviour and ideas. A set of tools for identifying and modelling human excellence, and a process for developing models, it has been simply defined as the study of excellence.

It is an extremely powerful tool, for providing understanding of human experience and activity. When it is used in therapeutic concerns, it can be an extremely effective technique for change in human behaviour and capacities, as well as improvement in communication. However as Richard Bandler has stated: *"NLP is not a set of techniques, it's an attitude"*[3].

NEUROLINGUISTIC PSYCHOTHERAPY

A ***constructivist*** therapy predicated in communication based upon trust and compassion. It utilises *skills* ***modelled*** and ***self-modelled*** from any therapeutic discipline by means of the ***structuralist*** and ***post-structuralist*** understandings of

NLP.

Richard Bandler says that NLP is a generative model. Clients who return for follow up sessions should be asking: *"What is possible for me and how can I go for it with enjoyment?"* rather than, *"What do I need to get over next?"*[16]

NEUROLOGICAL LEVELS
[See *Unified Field*]

NEUROLOGY
Comprising both our thought processes and our physiological procedures, the nervous system is one of the three components (the "N") of NLP. The basic building block of the nervous system is the *neurone*, countless millions of which constitute the nervous system. The neurone consists of the *soma* (or *cell body*), the *axon* (a nerve fibre that carries information from one neurone to another), and a *synapse* (a terminal junction at which the activity of one neurone influences the electrical characteristics of the soma of another).

Junctions between neurones occur either on the cell body itself or on tiny extensions of the cell body called *dendrites*.

Because we all possess these neurological patterns, we are able to share experiences, thus creating language and models and co-creating our common culture. We cannot be sure that our shared experiences correspond precisely, as we each have our own personal models of the world; our perceptions vary; what we perceive as reality is merely our (neurological) **model of reality**.

NEW CODE NLP
A reformulation of NLP within an ecological framework developed by **John Grinder** and **Judith DeLozier**. Unlike some **models** which attempt to achieve **outcomes** by programming from conscious awareness; New Code NLP recognises the wisdom of the **unconscious**.

To make an ecologically valid understanding from which to take action in the world, it is necessary to access three perceptual positions.. These are: First Position - being associated in my own body and feelings; Second Position - associating with the perceptions of a second person, group, family, community or any other living system; Third Position - watching the interaction between First and Second Positions from a comfortable observing location.

New Code NLP does not seek to integrate these positions, but rather to see them as a dynamic whole. Further positions may be introduced into the system, a fourth, for example may be constructed to ensure that third position is being truly comfortable and objective. The higher the *logical level* of observation, (and abstraction), the greater degree of control may be brought to bear on the system. *Fourth position* has also been defined as visceral knowledge of self in relation to others and relationship[10]. But no observing position may be truly independent of influence from the positions beneath it. In this way New Code NLP mirrors the idea that the individual (level 1) walks upon the world (level 2), which is supported on the back of a big turtle (level 3). After that, the story goes, "It is turtles all the way down".

New Code NLP borrows freely from several sources notably the writings of Carlos Castaneda. It defines two levels of awareness *first attention* and *second attention*. These are referred to by Castaneda as the **Tonal** and **Nagual** respectively. The Tonal grabs attention, categorises, objectifies and names the parts created. This includes naming the conceptualised nagual: 'The Nagual'. The Nagual, by contrast categorises nothing, but contains the Tonal within it. The Tonal is therefore at a lower logical level than the Nagual; and first attention or consciousness occupies a lower logical level than second attention which is undifferentiated. Second attention is limited in what it may perceive from the outside world by the interplay of afferent (incoming) and efferent (outgoing) tracking in our individual neurology. This can be quite complex. Our eyes for example have far more receptors in the retina than there are nerve fibres on the optic track. The richness of the interconnections of these receptors suggest that the eye may be 'intelligent', and may make distinctions about the world before communicating with second attention.

The implication is that *second attention* operating out of perception is processing much more information than the post-linguistic world of the *Tonal* and the *first attention* which operates within it. However, even *second attention* has limited access to the unknowable world of the *Nagual*, from which perceptions arise in a recursive manner.[9]

New Code NLP treats the concept of **parts** slightly differently from the traditional patterns of **reframing**, or **parts integration**. It actively encourages the creation of semiautonomous processes which can operate to perform specific functions. These specialists are called demons or demon states and perform with the same degree of compulsion as an archetype. However, within the New Code, controllers are also set up at a higher logical level than the demons. The controller's function being to mediate between conflicting demons, and to monitor the ecology of the individual and his environment. For example, the artist may be absorbed in painting for several hours with no awareness of time, but the controller will insure that s/he remembers to collect the children from school at the appropriate moment.

A controller, is not simply a new name for a punitive superego or nurturing parent though. The controller is an executive of second attention, and does not judge, chide or categorise in any way. It does not speak - it is quite simply, unconsciously aware. It intervenes smoothly by diverting energy from the demon state cleanly, and reallocates first attention to where it will be more ecologically valid.
[See *Turtles, Demons, Demon State*]

NOMINALIZATION
Using a process of linguistic distortion to change a verb into an abstract noun. The term is also used for the noun thus

formed. It takes a process and turns it into an event or a thing and, in so doing, nominalizations delete information and reduce choices. For example, when we change the verb "to be afraid" into the noun "fear" we create a nominalization.

"In this way you utterly confuse those around you and yourself - unless you remember that it is a representation rather than experience. This can have positive uses. If you happen to be a government, then you can talk about nominalizations like "national security" and you can get people to worry about those words. Our president just went to Egypt and changed the word "imperative" to the word "desirable" and suddenly we're friends with Egypt again. All he did was change a word. That's word magic."(2)

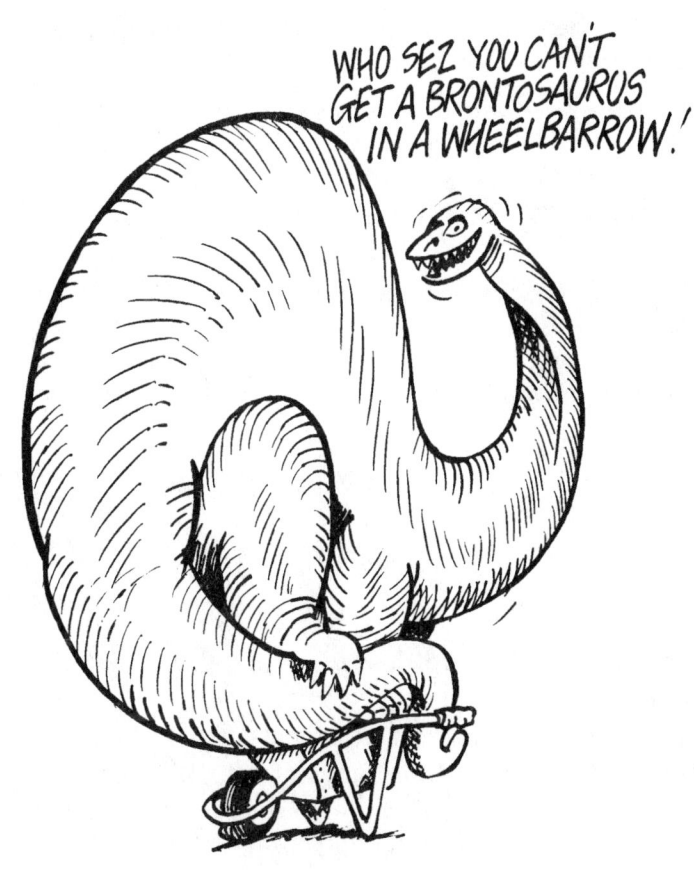

There are simple tests to determine whether a word is a nominalization. One such test is to imagine placing an adjective such as "constant" before the word. If the subsequent phrase makes sense, it is a nominalization. "Constant fear" makes sense; "constant afraid" or "constant being afraid" does not. Another test, which will determine whether the noun is abstract or concrete is to imagine putting it into a wheelbarrow. "Fear" would not fit sensibly into a wheelbarrow; an apple, a table, a brontosaurus (if the wheelbarrow were large enough) would.

Nominalizations may be processed using a pattern which puts the activity, which has been distorted into an object, back into the statement as a process, (or verb):

A. I broke off the relationship

B. In what ways were you relating to whom and about what?

[See *Meta Model*]

OLFACTORY
Pertaining to the sense of smell.

ORGANIC SYSTEM
[See *Natural System*]

ORIENTATION
The direction towards which a ***sensory system*** is orientated. The possibilities are (^{e}) external; (^{i}) internal; (^{i}) remembered and (^{c}) constructed.
[See *TOTE Notation*]

OUTCOMES
Specific, sensory-based desired results that meet clearly formulated criteria.

An outcome is what I want, described in terms of the senses, or ***representational systems***. Thus it has to be stated in terms of how I want to see, hear and feel when I've got it - and, if appropriate, what I will smell and taste. Unless I know precisely what I want, I am unlikely to achieve it and, more significantly, unlikely to know if I have achieved it.

Outcomes need to be stated in a positive way. What I want, not what I don't want. My outcome may be to write a book. I express this, therefore as "I will write a book," not "I will stop finding excuses for not writing a book." Outcomes also need to be concrete in content and in tone, attainable, and ecologically sound. Outcomes differ from goals. An outcome has to be specific; a goal need not be specific.

Formulating outcomes is a method used in NLP to achieve changes in our lives by determining what are our goals and desires. There are a number of questions we can ask to determine our desired states or outcomes:

What precisely do I want?
Have I described it in positive terms?
How will I know when I have got it?
What will I be doing, feeling, seeing, thinking, tasting, or smelling when I have got it?
How will I look when I have achieved my outcome?
With whom will I be sharing my outcome?
What will be the difference between what I want and what I have at present?
Will my outcome be ecologically sound and acceptable to me and to any others whom it may affect?

[*It could also be useful to identify traits or patterns which I might allow to deflect me from my efforts to achieve my outcome.*]

Outcomes may be long-term or short-term. A short-term outcome expresses what I want at the present time; in the here and now. A long-term outcome is what I want to achieve in the future.

Successful **negotiation** consists of knowing what I want (i.e. my outcome), finding out what the other person wants (i.e. their outcome), and dovetailing our outcomes so that we both achieve a positive result.

[See *Dovetailing Outcomes*]

OUTPUT CHANNELS
The ways in which a person communicates. Language is only one of these, and (in NLP terms) one of the poorest. Other channels of communication include breathing, posture, body language, tonality, tempo and gestures.

OVERLAP
The use of one *representational system* to access another. For example I might use a piece of music to recall a scene from the past; or I might visualise a scene from the past in order to recall something that was said at the time.
[See also *Chaining Anchors, Failure into Feedback, Synesthesias*]

PACING
A means of achieving and maintaining *rapport* with another person, on both the conscious and unconscious levels, by matching their behaviour both verbally and non-verbally.

Techniques used include matching predicates, matching voice tone and tempo, mirroring, leading, switching and *strategies*.

"HE'S JUST TAKEN A COURSE OF BALLROOM DANCING LESSONS"

Direct mirroring, one type of non-verbal pacing, involves matching the rate and depth of one's breathing to that of the other person. The effect on them will be profound, even though they may be totally unaware of what is being done. Another way is by ***cross-over mirroring***, either in the same ***representational system*** or by switching systems.

An example of the former technique is to match a physical movement, say the nodding of one's head, or the tapping of a pencil, to the breathing rhythm of the other person. The latter could be achieved by matching our speech tempo to the other person's rate of breathing.

Successful pacing can enable the practitioner to join the other person in their representation of the world, and then, by changing what they are doing, lead them into a new behaviour.

[See *Matching, Mirroring, Leading, Predicates, Switching*]

PARAMESSAGES

Messages of the same **logical level** expressed in different **output channels**. With a congruent communication, each of the paramessages (language, posture, tonality, breathing, etc.) matches each of the others. With an incongruent communication, one or more of the paramessages will not fit or be congruent with each of the others.

Visual paramessages are conveyed by the position of head, hands, feet, legs, neck, etc., and by facial expression, eye patterns, and breathing. Auditory paramessages are conveyed by words and phraseology used, by speech tempo, voice volume, and by patterns of intonation.

[See *Congruence, Incongruence, R-Operator*]

PARTS

Separate semiautonomous areas of our personality, each of which seeks its own form of nurturing, sometimes setting up a conflict with another subpersonality, or part. In order to change the behaviour pattern resulting from this conflict, it is necessary to establish precisely why any one part may be upset: e.g. the part which makes us quit trying, or procrastinate, or develop a headache whenever we have an important meeting.

As a rule the intention behind any one part's behaviour, even when apparently negative, is to protect us. If we can establish the specific intent of the conflicting part, we can find another way to satisfy it by *reframing*. Once we have satisfied the intent, we can again function congruently.

[See *Congruence* and *Incongruence*]

PATTERN-INTERRUPTS

Interrupting a normal behaviour pattern can have a very drastic effect on *rapport* and is therefore to be treated with caution. Starting to shake someone's hand, and then suddenly withdrawing your hand; suddenly getting up from your chair and walking away as someone is talking to you; abruptly closing your eyes as something is being shown to you; all these interruptions of accustomed patterns of behaviour can be very confusing.

The psychiatrist **Dr. Milton H. Erickson** created a method for inducing hypnosis which he called the confusion technique which was based upon this notion. The confusion occurs because, within the concept of the *TOTE*, individuals may sense ("T") and operate ("O") as a sequence, but are interrupted before they are able to test the effectiveness of their *strategy* ("T") and are therefore unable to exit ("E"). Within this short space of time, an individual is susceptible to suggestion as they are searching inside and outside themselves for information with which to make sense of the situation, within the *context* of their *map of reality*.

When achieved in rapport, pattern interruption may be used constructively to influence, as in therapeutic *hypnosis* and *family therapy*.

[See *Patterns of Behaviour, TOTE, TOTE Notation*]

PATTERNS OF BEHAVIOUR

A pattern of behaviour is a sequence of habitual responses such as shaking the hand that is offered to you, or sitting in a chair that is being held back for you.

[See *Context Markers, Pattern-Interrupts*]

PERCEPTUAL FILTERS

Our *model of the world* is shaped by our experiences, our beliefs, the ideas that we absorb, and, above all, by *language*. These are the perceptual filters that define the uniqueness of our world compared with that of another person.

Perceptual filters are determined by *neurological constraints* and *social constraints* such as culture and *personal history*. A nice example comes from Mark Twain's Huckleberry Finn:

"Looky here, Jim; does a cat talk like we do?"
"No, a cat don't."
"Well, does a cow?"
"No, a cow don't, nuther."
"Does a cat talk like a cow, or a cow talk like a cat?"
"No, dey don't."
"It's natural and right for 'em to talk different from each other, ain't it?"
"Course."
"And ain't it natural and right for a cat and a cow to talk different from us?"

"Why, mos' sholy it is."
"Well, then, why ain't it natural and right for a Frenchman to talk different from us? You answer me that."
"Is a cat a man, Huck?"
"No."
"Well, den, dey ain't no sense in a cat talkin' like a man. Is a cow a man? - er is a cow a cat?"
"No, she ain't neither of them."
"Well den, she ain' got no business to talk like either one er the yuther of 'em. Is a Frenchman a man?"
"Yes."
"Well, den! Dad blame it, why doan' he talk like a man? You answer me dat!"
[Also known as *Constraints*]

PERCEPTUAL POSITION
The point of view we take at any time may be our own (See ***First Position***), that of another (See ***Second Position***), or that of an observer (See ***Third Position***), or visceral sensing of the complete system (See ***Fourth Position***).
[See *Triple Description*]

PERLS, FREDERICK S.
One of the three major influences, as models, in the development of NLP [the other two being **Virginia Satir** and **Milton Erickson**].

Frederick S. (Fritz) Perls (1893-1970) was one of the founders of ***gestalt therapy***, a technique of personal integration based on the idea that all of nature is a unified and coherent whole, and in order to achieve the illusion of differentiation this whole splits into two components. These are defined as a distinct and interesting *figure* set against a less distinct and uninteresting *background*.

Fritz Perls possessed an intuitive skill in helping people to achieve dramatic personality changes, leading to more positive behaviour patterns. In later years he became known for his work in negotiating between conflicting ***parts***. The

NLP process of *reframing* owes much to Perls' technique of eliciting the function those parts served for the individual, as well as how they limited a person's response-ability.
[Works include: *Ego, Hunger and Aggression, Gestalt Therapy Verbatim,* and *In and Out of the Garbage Pail*.]

PERSONAL HISTORY
The conscious and unconscious encoding of the past from conception to the present day. Our ability to access and make sense of this will be constrained by the limitations of human perception, the effect of language, family and culture.

PHOBIA CURE
A technique for the rapid elimination of strong fears or phobias, by utilising *dissociation*, enabling the subject to view events in perspective, such as being the audience of a scene on a cinema screen rather than being in the scene itself.
[See *Change History*]

PHONOLOGICAL AMBIGUITY
Words of similar sound, but different meanings, e.g. principle and principal, or great and grate.

PHYSIOLOGY
Pertaining to an individual's physical aspect. Physiology, in the NLP context, comprises the way we breathe, our posture and body language, our facial expressions and skin tone. Also our physical health, neurology and self care.

Said to be one of the two royal roads to understanding working with *states*. The other being *mind* .

PLACATOR
Individuals who attempt to keep everyone happy because disagreements make them feel uncomfortable (K^1). They are said to be dependent upon others to motivate and provide them with a sense of self, (or self-esteem).
[See *Satir, Virginia*]

POSITIVE LINKING
[See *Linking*]

PREDICATE PATTERNS
The correct identification of predicate patterns helps us to understand how information is being processed. One way to achieve and maintain ***rapport*** is by matching predicate patterns: by consciously choosing ***predicates*** which match those of another person, it is possible to accomplish much clearer and more direct communication with that person.

  Some examples:
 1. I see what you mean (Visual)
    That's music to my ears (Auditory)
    I feel sympathetic (Kinaesthetic)
    to that viewpoint (Visual)
    [All of which mean:
    I agree with you]
 2. Let me show you this (Visual)

Just listen to what I have to tell you (Auditory)
Try and grasp this (Kinaesthetic)
All of which mean:
 I'd like to communicate something to you]
3. That really looks good (Visual)
Sounds great to me (Auditory)
It feels absolutely marvellous (Kinaesthetic)
[All of which mean:
We have achieved rapport about that]

PREDICATES

Sensory-based words, such as descriptive verbs, adverbs, and adjectives which correspond to visual, auditory or kinaesthetic representations, are designated predicates. These are words that we use to describe those aspects of our experiences which correspond to the processes and relationships in the experiences.

The habitual use of one type of sensory-based predicate is a good indication of a person's preferred *representational system*, within a specific context. Thus "I see how you did that" or "I get the picture" would indicate a visual representation; "I hear what you say" or "That strikes the right note" are typical of auditory representation; while "he takes a hard line" or "she's a cool customer" would be kinaesthetic; and "that's a bitter pill to swallow" or "it smells fishy to me" are indicative of gustatory/olfactory predicate preference.

PREFERRED REPRESENTATION SYSTEM

The *representational system* (auditory, kinaesthetic, visual) which is most habitually used to process someone's experiences. It is the system in which people make most distinctions about themselves and their environments.

PRESENT STATE
[See *Stuck State*]

PRESUPPOSITIONS

In a language system a presupposition is a meaning hidden within a *deep structure* which must be true if the *surface structure* is to make sense. Presuppositions are basic assumptions that we make and expect to be taken for granted when communicating.

Very often "why" questions precede a presupposition, as do statements beginning with "if" or "when". "Why don't you think of me sometimes?" makes the assumption that you do not think of me. "When you grow up, you'll understand what I mean." In other words, you do not understand what I mean. "If you had more sense you'd see what you're doing to me," is another way of saying that "you don't have much sense".

Presuppositions are a form of *mind reading*; they are the cause of much misunderstanding, and may be countered by the response: "How do you know that. . .?" or "What makes you think I don't. . .?" Thus: "How do you know I don't think of you?", and "What makes you think I don't understand?"

NLP is predicated on a number of presuppositions.
[See *Presuppositions of NLP, Transformational Grammar*]

PRESUPPOSITIONS OF NLP

These presuppositions have been formulated in various ways. However, their effect is to provide a *deep structure*, by which NLP may be understood, rather than by providing a more basic *surface structure* definition.

Model Making: Human beings are able to discriminate between different experiences and behaviour on the basis of what they see, hear, feel, taste and smell.

These sensory experiences are shaped into a model of the world through the processes of deletion, distortion and generalisation.

The map, or model is not the territory, (or what is occurring or was occurring, or will occur).

There are no substitutes for clean, open sensory channels,

and direct sensory-specific information you get from them.
Responses: *A person cannot "not communicate". Seeming not to respond is communication at a higher level.*

You will always get a response to a communication in so far as you are observant and perceptive enough to notice it. It is useful to believe that the meaning of a communication is the response you receive, rather than what you hoped to communicate.

No progress can be made without rapport. If you are not receiving the co-operation you require then you are not in rapport and need to *pace* the other person.

Change: There is no failure, only feedback.

People already have in their history all the resources necessary to make any desired change.

There is a positive intention behind all our parts and all our behaviour.

The positive worth of any individual is of paramount importance; their values, or the appropriateness of their behaviour may be questioned.

PUNCTUATION AMBIGUITY

It is possible to give an example of one can always recognise it by the way two sentences merge.

RAPPORT

The state of greatest responsive interaction between two or more people. Also the process of establishing and maintaining that state, and generating trust and understanding. It can occur naturally and spontaneously, as in an intimate relationship, or it can be achieved deliberately by *mirroring* and *matching*.

One of the great fallacies in interaction is the belief that other people have the same map [see **Model of the World**] as we do. The essence of achieving rapport with another person is to maintain total flexibility of language, tonality, breathing patterns, and gestures, while recognising that the onus for successful communication is upon ourselves.

Failure to convey a message is failure to communicate; gaining rapport is a guarantee of successful communication, and the ability to establish rapport is a significant skill. In a *negotiation* the presence of rapport is a vital element in the achievement of both parties' *outcomes*; the absence of rapport is a good guide to the probable failure of attainment of your outcomes.
[See *Pacing, Matching Predicates, Mirroring, Switching, Leading*]

REFERENCE STRUCTURE
The totality of experiences in a person's life history. It is also the most complete representation within a system from which other representations are derived; thus the *deep structure* serves as the *reference structure* for **surface structure**.
[See *Personal History, Timelines*]

REFERENT
A word usefully defined by Ogden and Richards[17], as the object or situation in the real world to which the word or label refers. The object of *semantics* is the establishment of the referent.

REFRAMING
Finding a different way of looking at a situation in order to give it another interpretation. R.D. Laing* gave some amusing examples of reframing.

Instead of displaying a negative behaviour pattern because I suffer from insomnia, he suggested, I can welcome the advantages of requiring so little sleep, since most people sleep too easily and too long, and waste much time that could be more usefully spent. This is an example of **content reframing** which can be identified by such a question as *"What if I tried doing..."*

Laing also described the situation of a catatonic female patient, who tended to fall into a catatonic trance "at the drop of a hat". She subsequently found a employment as an artists' model, thus making a profitable career of her catatonia. This is an example of **context reframing** and can be identified by such a question as: *"Where might this be more appropriate...?"*

Reframing thus changes negative behaviour into positive behaviour, and negative perceptions into positive perceptions. When we reframe our behaviour patterns it is known as a complex reframe; when we reframe our perception of another person's behaviour, or an external circumstance, it is known as a simple reframe.

Richard Bandler and **John Grinder**[1] designed a six-part reframing outline to aid changes in unwanted behaviour patterns while, at the same time, retaining those parts of the old behaviour which are of benefit.
[See *Six Step Reframing*]
*In the course of a seminar, subsequently televised as *"Didn't You Used To Be R.D. Laing?"*

RE-IMPRINTING

A powerful pattern for re-authoring a significant experience from the past during which a person formed a belief or a complex of beliefs. This experience usually results in unconscious role modelling of significant others, (leading to cultural transmission of the problem). Re-imprinting updates the role models by restoring to them the human qualities filtered from their *capabilities* by virtue of their own cultural programming and *personal history*:

1. Identify the *Four Tuple* associated with the belief or complex of beliefs.
2. Step out of the experience and identify the characters who surrounded the individual at the time contributing to the formation of the complex of beliefs.
3. Ask the least significant character what the positive intention of their action was.
4. Determine what resources this character seemed to lack which, if available, would have enabled them to meet their positive intention in a way which would have led you to form positive beliefs and or capabilities.
5. From your *personal history*, find a counter-example when you had access to this resource. Associate into this experiencing all the representations of it (i.e. the *four tuple*). Anchor these and transfer them to the character concerned.
6. Recycle to Step 3 for the next least significant actor until all have been treated similarly.
7. Locate the resource that would have enabled you to have created a different complex of beliefs in the *original circumstances*. This is achieved by following step 5.
8. From a dissociated position re-create all the characters in the original situation, making sure that the extra resources necessary for their helpful support are present. Also re-create yourself as a person with all the personal strength needed to face the original situation.
9. When the scene looks healthy and harmonious, step into the body of yourself at that age, surrounded as you are by all these resourceful people, and slowly grow up from that point

in time. Pay special attention to how later challenging situations and decisions in your life have subtly changed.

10. Future pace by placing yourself in an imagined challenging situation in the future and examine how you might react. Ensure that the resources added by the re-imprinting pattern are all available to you in the imagined future situation.

[See *Engram, Future Pacing, Re-authoring*]

RELATIONAL OPERATOR
See *R-Operator*.

RELEVANCY CHALLENGE
A technique whereby querying the relevancy of a statement makes it possible to avoid deviation from a topic in conversation. For example by asking: "What has that particular statement to do with the matter we're discussing?"

REMEDIAL TECHNIQUES
Techniques which have the aim of producing a specific outcome in a particular context. Such techniques include *anchoring*, *reimprinting*, and *dissociation*.

REPRESENTATION
An image of something which is different from the thing itself.
[Also called a *map* or a *model*]

REPRESENTATIONAL SYSTEMS
How we code sensory information in our minds. The use of the five senses [*visual, auditory, kinaesthetic, olfactory, gustatory*] to absorb, sort, store, and use information obtained both externally and internally.

Representational systems have been described as *"other maps for the same territory"*[10], but our representational systems use the three processes of *generalisation*, *deletion* and *distortion* to modify the territory they model.

The five senses (or ***input channels***) receive information from an external or internal source and then store that information in a ***map*** or ***model*** which may differ from the channel by which it entered. For example, I may hear the sound of my microwave oven as it heats a bowl of chilli, and convert this auditory knowledge to the visual image of the lighted oven, with the chilli bubbling away inside.

In similar vein, I might read a menu and actually taste (say a tandoori chicken) to the extent that I start salivating. But the menu is not the meal!

Bandler and ***Grinder***[10] have stated that *"the way that each of us represents our experience will either cause us pain or allow us an exciting, living and growing process in our lives. More specifically, if we choose (consciously or not) to represent certain kinds of experience in one or another of our representational systems, we will succeed either in causing ourselves pain, or in giving ourselves new choices*

RIGHT! IT'S DINNER AT THE BELLE EPOCH.

It is considered that pain caused by an experience represented in one system may be dealt with effectively if it is switched to the system which the sufferer most typically uses to represent the world and his/her experience of it. [See also: *Six Step Reframing*]

RESOURCEFUL STATE

The total neurological and physical experience constituting a feeling that you can achieve a desired outcome. An optimum state of psychological excellence.

It is possible to model a resourceful state by accessing a time when you were actually in such a state and then *anchoring* the experience.

Thus, you might recall a specific occasion when you had the exhilarating experience of some extraordinarily well-accomplished achievement, recapture the memory of what you saw at that time, what you felt at that time, what you heard at that time (what you smelled and tasted at that time, if those senses were significant), and then touch a part of your body, or tap your knee, or squeeze your hands together at the moment when the past experience is most vividly recalled. [*Having someone else anchor the resource state at the right moment is even more powerful.*] Then, whenever the physical "anchor" is repeated you access the resourceful state.

[*In the cartoon illustrating the note on* anchoring *, the little boy might have been expected to access the feeling of successful homework every time his head is patted*!]

Another method of "anchoring" is to imagine a "circle of excellence" on the floor. Now recall the time when you did something exceptionally well. Step into the circle and you step into your resourceful state at the moment of supreme achievement. If you then access all your *sensory-based experiences* of that time and relive them, as well as being aware of your behavioural patterns while reliving the earlier experience [*even better is to have someone observe changes in your physical appearance and changes in your facial expression as you re-experience the moment of exhilaration, and* **match** *and* **mirror** *them*], you can recapture the resourceful state at any time by stepping back into the imaginary circle and re-accessing the feelings, body language and facial expressions. A further anchoring device is to find a word to describe your feelings when you are in the circle,

and use that word in conjunction with the circle when you next wish to recapture the state.
[See *State of Excellence*]

RESOURCES
Those experiences, states or strategies which enable you to achieve an *outcome* .

Resources may be internal or external. Internal resources might include such emotional states as persistence, love, humour, and confidence. Strictly speaking these are non-specific complex-equivalent ***nominalizations***. External resources might comprise physical skills, strength, speed of reflex, etc.

To access resources you could ask yourself the question: "What personal resources to I need to achieve my outcome?" This could then be reinforced by the "as-if" method, i.e. imagining that the outcome is achieved and asking yourself: "How did I do it? What did I do next?" An alternative is to imagine someone else, real or imaginary, who has achieved the desired outcome, and then try to visualise yourself acting the part of that person.

It is also helpful to think back to a time in your past when you were particularly successful at something. Then, closing your eyes, and reviewing the accomplishment in the largest, clearest, and brightest images, access your feelings, visualise your physical appearance, and recall any associated sounds, smells, or tastes at that time; after which the presently desired outcome could be visualised within the same referential frames.

RESPONSES
A person cannot *not* respond. Even appearing not to respond is a response at a different ***logical level***.

You will always get an answer to a question to the extent that you have developed the acuity of your five senses to notice it. [See ***Sensory Acuity***]

Resistance is a comment about the lack of flexibility of

the communicator rather than that of the recipient. If a communication results in a response which is different from what was expected, it suggests that although *rapport* may have been achieved with the other person, a variation of the form of communication will be needed. Language is generally a poor form of communication unless it is translated into the representational system of the other person and presented congruently.
[See *Congruence*]

ROLE MODEL
Mnemonic device denoting: ***Representational System***; ***Orientation***; ***Linkage*** and ***Effect***. This is one of the simplest and most effective ways of coding information about how an individual is thinking.

SATIR, VIRGINIA
Pioneer of Conjoint Family Therapy and co-founder of the Mental Research Institute of Palo Alto, California, the late Virginia Satir's methods and personal style had a profound influence on **Richard Bandler** and **John Grinder**, for whom she was one of their three major models in their development of NLP [the others being **Fritz Perls** and **Milton Erickson**.

"*If you watch and listen to Virginia Satir work you are confronted with an overwhelming mass of information - the way she moves, her voice tone, the way she touches, who she turns to next, what sensory cues she is using to orient herself to which member of the family...*

"*Now we don't know what Virginia Satir really does with families. However we can describe her behaviour in such a way that we can come to any of you and say "Here. Take this. do these things in sequence. Practice until it becomes a systematic part of your unconscious behaviour, and you will end up being able to elicit the same responses that Virginia elicits"...*

"*After being exposed to it and practising the patterns and the descriptions that we have offered, people's behaviour changes in ways that make them effective in the same way Satir is, yet each person's style is unique. If you learn to speak French, you will still express yourself in your own way."* (2)

Some of the theoretical concepts central to Satir's work are self-worth, rules, and systems. Self-worth determines our right to be "where we're at"; it is how we acknowledge our importance to ourselves and take responsibility for ourselves. We can choose the "rules" which we wish to follow rather than those we "should" obey as a mark of our autonomy. And the successful functioning of systems is dependent upon our developing into a whole person.

Another significant contribution by Satir was her categorising of behaviour patterns, identifying them by means of the postural stances that people displaying them tend to adopt, and then exaggerating them to make them readily identifiable. The four types distinguished by Satir are the **Placator**, the **Blamer**, the **Computer**, and the **Distracter**. They are all characterised by body posture, gestures, body sensations, and syntax. All the Satir types are caricatures of preferred *representational systems* and the defences associated with each of these.

The Placator is trying to keep everyone happy, in order to be loved, and in that aim will take the blame for things going wrong; the placator's key word is "agree"; the placator is a "yes-person".

The Blamer believes that he is always right unless he yells, no one will accept his model of the world. As a result inside he feels lonely and unsuccessful.

The Computer believes that by being "super-reasonable" he will show people how smart he really is; his body language suggests calmness and correctness, but inside he feels vulnerable.

The Distractor will indulge in irrelevancies in order to get noticed, even when the words make no sense and when the behaviour pattern is way off beam; they are actually telling themselves that nobody wants them.

[Books include: *Changing with Families* with Richard Bandler and John Grinder, *Conjoint Family Therapy, Peoplemaking, Making Contact*]

SCORE MODEL
A model devised by **Robert Dilts** and Todd Epstein during the 1980s. The Mnemonic stands for: **S**ymptoms, **C**auses, **O**utcome, **R**esources and **E**ffects.

SECOND POSITION
The second of three *perceptual positions*. The position in which we look at the world from another person's point of view.
[See *New Code NLP, Triple Description*]

SECONDARY GAIN
An indirect payoff associated with a state or pattern of behaviour that may be considered undesirable. Such a benefit may be accidental and the purpose served by it unconscious. Thus, though the behaviour may be recognised as being disadvantageous, the secondary gain may provide a positive benefit. From this concept comes the conclusion that any behaviour, no matter how bizarre, serves a useful purpose at some level, even if the purpose is unconscious.

SEMANTICS
The study of meaning. A way to make language a better vehicle for communication. *"Grammar, syntax, dictionary derivations, are to semantics as a history of the coinage is to the operations going on in a large modern bank"* [11].

There are two major language violations: the identification of words with things, and the misuse of abstract words. In the phrase "This is a dog", the thing that is called dog is a non-verbal object. It can be observed by the senses, it can be described and then, for convenience, the label 'dog' can be attached to it. *But the label is not the animal.*

"We are continually confusing the label with the non-verbal

object and so giving a spurious validity to the word, as something alive and barking in its own right. When this tendency to identify expands from dogs to higher abstractions such as 'liberty', 'justice', 'the eternal', and imputes living breathing entity to them, almost nobody knows what anybody else means. . ."[11]

There are three rough classes of labels for things. First there are the labels for common objects like dog or table. Here there is no great problem of understanding. Secondly come labels for groups and classes of things, such as mankind, America, lawyers, which are abstractions, and where their use often leads to confusion. Finally we have labels for essences and qualities, such as freedom, individualism, truth, labour, for which there are no **referents** in the outside world. These concepts belong to the world of philosophy, politics and economics and are, perhaps, best left there.

"On the level of simple directions, commands, descriptions, the difficulty is not great. When the words mean 'look out!', 'there is your food', 'go to the next white house and turn left', communication is clear. But when we hear words on the level of ideas and generalisations, we cheer loudly, we grow angry, and we storm the barricades - and often we do not know what the other man is saying."[11]

SENSORY ACUITY

The ability to be aware of **sensory feedback**. Making use of visual, auditory, kinaesthetic, olfactory/gustatory information obtained externally to create **sensory-based descriptions**. We are able to estimate another person's emotional state by careful observation of changes in muscle tone, skin colour, breathing patterns, eye movements, and the lower lip. These changes are often very subtle.

Sensory acuity is a very useful skill in establishing **rapport** and in aiding communication. Observing minute sensory changes is a valuable talent in **negotiations** and in **dovetailing outcomes**.

There is no substitute for clean open sensory specific

information of what we see, hear, feel, taste and smell.
[See also *Calibration*]

SENSORY-BASED DESCRIPTION
The use of words to describe, but not to diagnose, an observation or experience directly verified by the senses of sight, sound, feeling, smell or taste. Thus: "His eyes are focused; his voice is raised and tremulous; his jaw is clenched tightly," provide a sensory-based description. The alternative statement: "He is angry", is interpretative or diagnostic; it is also known as *mind reading*.

SENSORY-BASED EXPERIENCE
An experience that is processed and may be interpreted on the level of what can be seen, heard, felt, smelled, and/or tasted.

SENSORY CODING
Those codes which are used to simplify references to the *sensory systems*. VAK(OG) is the acronym usually employed for the aggregate of the Visual, Auditory, Kinaesthetic, Olfactory, and Gustatory senses.

Detailed examples of coding are amplified under the heading **TOTE Notation**.
[See also *Eye Accessing Cues*]

SENSORY FEEDBACK
The information we get back from the world through out senses.
[See *New Code NLP*]

SENSORY MAP
The representation of an experience which utilises the senses by, for instance, remembering how one felt at the time, what one saw at the time, what one heard, smelled or tasted at the time, etc.

SENSORY SET
The combination of the five sensory systems: visual, auditory, kinaesthetic, and olfactory/gustatory.
[See *TOTE*]

SENSORY SYSTEMS
The systems that enable us to see, hear, feel, taste and smell.

SEVEN C's MODEL
An idea proposed by **Robert Dilts** and Todd Epstein in the 1980s. The Seven C's comprise 'interference' the factors that get in the way of achieving goals:
Confusion - Lack of clarity, vision or the steps needing to be taken.
[See *Meta Model*]
Content - Inappropriate materials, inputs, concepts. In cybernetic terms 'Garbage in garbage out'.
[See *Relevancy Filter, Sensory Acuity*]
Catastrophes - Negative imprints from personal history.
[See *Anchoring, Dissociation, Change History, Re-imprinting*]
Comparison - Inappropriate expectations and criteria.
[See *Chunking, Modelling*]
Conflict - Hidden Agendas, Incongruency.
[See *Negotiation, Reframing, Rapport*]
Context - External constraints.
[See *Sensory Acuity, Behavioural Demonstration*]
Conviction - Doubt about achieving the goal.
[See *Future Pacing, Swish Pattern*]

SEVEN - THE MAGICAL NUMBER
George Miller in his paper *"The Magical Number Seven Plus or Minus Two: Some Limits to our capacity for processing information"* (Psychological Review, 63, March 1956) suggests that the human mind is able to retain only seven, plus or minus two, chunks of information in consciousness.
[See *Deletion, Chunking*]

SINGLE SENTENCE REFRAMING

A method of changing the meaning or the context of a particular stimulus, by giving an alternative (positive) meaning to a negative statement, or by placing a negative statement in an alternative (positive) context.

For example: "I can never do that properly," might be reframed to the subject as: "I hear (see/understand) what you are saying. You know, you will have a wonderful feeling when you do succeed in doing it properly." Or: "I see (hear/understand) what you mean. Can you remember a time when you felt the same way, but actually managed to achieve it?" [See *Reframing*]

SIX STEP REFRAMING

A way of negotiating between parts which enables the function, or positive intention of a part to be maintained whilst changing its behaviour or effect.

1. Identify the *part* of your personality (the subpersonality) which is causing the unwanted behaviour, and identify the pattern to be changed.
2. Establish communication with the part responsible for the pattern.
3. Distinguish between the unwanted behaviour and the intention of the part responsible for the behaviour.
4. Create at least three new behaviours to satisfy the intention.
5. Ask the part to accept responsibility for generating the three new options in the appropriate context.
6. Check that the alternatives are ecologically acceptable; if another part objects to the alternatives, it will be necessary to recycle to step 2.

SIZZLE

A flirtatious state attributed to the teachings of **Richard Bandler** by Michael Head[18]. The purpose of 'Sizzle' is not lust or promiscuity; but rather to access the natural resource of smiling, being friendly, treating people with respect, letting them know that you like them, having a tune in your mind as you greet another human being!

SLEIGHT OF MOUTH PATTERNS
A set of alternative structures for decoupling *cause-effect* statements and *reframing* them.

SOCIAL SYSTEM
[See *Human Activity System*]

SPIRIT
A logical level above *identity*. Something greater than oneself. The gateway to the Divine. A connectedness, or transfiguration with the natural world; other realms and the cosmos.
[See *Logical Levels*]

STATE
The aggregation of our neurological processes at any one time. The mood we are in; our affect. This operates at the capability level within **Robert Dilt's** concept of **unified field theory**. Our state will influence our perception of an experience at any one moment in time, and our interpretation of it.

Changing state is a naturally occuring phenomenon, but may be purposely programmed. Accessing the feelings and the behavioural patterns of our positive states is a powerful way to dissipate a negative state. Learning how to adopt physical poses which are associated with our positive behaviour patterns is another way of changing state. It is helpful to have another person study our "body language" when we are in a particularly powerful positive state, and then have us adopt the same posture when we are feeling negative as a means of changing state. This can be reinforced if the other person also tries *matching* or *mirroring* our body language.

A useful exercise, which enables us to change the negative internal auditory messages we give ourselves, is to imagine

we are hearing them on a radio, then imagine ourselves slowly turning down the volume control until the voice becomes a mere murmur. This sound can then be replaced by pleasant or joyful sounds, and positive messages.
[See also *Auditory Tapes, Break State, Resourceful State, State of Excellence*]

STATE ALTERATION
The 'drifting' of intensity and representation of *state* due to the influence of immediate experience.

STATE AWARENESS
As states drift out of consciousness they need periodic re-calibration. It is desirable to set up a ***controller***, as a reminder of the need to bring a state back into consciousness for this purpose.
[See *Calibration, Learning Theory*]

STATE DEPENDENCY
As states are associated with ***anchoring, context*** and ***physiology***, the imbibing of drugs and or alcohol will affect an individual's ability to perceive the phenomenal world. An individual experiencing an emotive event when in such a state, may be unable to recall the experience in a 'normal' state of consciousness. However, if reoriented into the 'altered' state then the memory is more likely to be intact. This is known as State Dependent Memory and Learning Behaviour [19].

STATE OF EXCELLENCE
That state in we feel at our best: our most positive, our happiest, our most confident. Possibly a time of exceptional achievement. An interesting and useful experiment is to have someone match and mirror our behavioural patterns while we are demonstrating a state of excellence (by reliving the experience, recalling the associated sensory stimuli), to enable us to return to such a state at will, by repeating the

patterns of behaviour associated with it.

To recall our state of excellence, our resourceful state, is to reproduce a state in which we can operate most effectively. To learn how to access this condition is to provide ourselves with a powerful tool for dealing with difficult situations, exploiting our most positive behaviour patterns, and getting "unstuck".
[See *Matching, Mirroring, Sensory Based Experience*]

STEPPING

Also known as ***chunking***, this is a way of changing our perception of a thing or a situation by moving up or down a level; in effect, changing ***generalisations*** into specifics.
[See *Logical Levels*]

"NOW I KNOW I'M SUPPOSED TO TAKE ONE STEP AT A TIME, BUT WHERE DO I START?"

STRATEGY

A sequence of behaviour patterns intended to produce a specific outcome; the way we organise our ideas and behaviour in order to perform a task. We can duplicate results by accessing a strategy - thus, we follow a knitting pattern to produce a sweater, or we copy a recipe to cook a dish.

It is possible to elicit a person's strategy by asking relevant questions and observing verbal and non-verbal response, such as *submodalities*, or eye movements.
[See *Eye Accessing Cues*].

STRESS AND TENSION
A potent factor in determining how an individual will respond in certain situations. Stress or tension might cause a person to retreat into a *preferred system* which will serve to restrict their response choices and smother their external awareness.

STRONG FEAR ELIMINATOR
[See *Phobia Cure*]

STUCK STATE
A negative or undesirable physiological-psychological state.

SUBMODALITIES
The components that make up each modality or *representational system*, enabling our brains to sort and code our experiences. Thus our visual submodality can be coded as to distance, depth, colour, lustre, size etc.; our auditory submodality has volume, tone, pitch, rhythm, tempo etc.; our kinaesthetic submodality comprises such perceptions as texture, pressure, temperature, intensity, etc.

Using our submodalities enables us to alter our perceptions of things. Recalling a past experience and making it brighter or louder, dimmer or softer, will change the way we feel about it. Increasing brightness, for example, will tend to make the feeling more intense; decreasing the brightness will also decrease the intensity of the recalled experience.

SURFACE STRUCTURE
The spoken or written part of communication, deriving from the *deep structure*, using the processes of *generalisation*, *deletion* and *distortion*.

SWISH PATTERN
The Swish Pattern is an unusual technique which uses the brain's natural rapid learning ability to achieve a result without specifying exactly how it is done. **Richard Bandler** once considered it to have *"a more powerful effect than any other technique I've used"*.[3]

The first step is to identify the behaviour or response that needs to be changed. An example could be the desire to stop smoking, or to eat less. The subject then identifies a specific cue that is associated with the condition, and makes a mental picture, as if on a cinema screen, of what they see immediately before entering the behaviour pattern which it is desired to change. The picture should then be expanded in size and brightness, and should be seen through the subject's own eyes, i.e. using **association**. This will produce a negative and unpleasant sensory feedback. If not, the subject should generate even more undesirable sensory perceptions associated with the condition.

Next the subject creates an **outcome** picture of how they would see themselves if the problem no longer existed. This should also be big and bright, it should be as attractive as possible to the subject, and should use **dissociation**. This will produce positive and pleasant sensory feedback which may be enhanced by the use of **anchoring**. The picture may be expanded, made brighter, and the positive aspects of the outcome should be stressed.

Then comes the swish. The subject goes back to the original, the cue picture, making it a really large, bright, associated image. As the subject views the cue picture, they place a small and dull image of the outcome picture in the centre of the screen. This small image will rapidly brighten and expand to fill the screen; it will stay dissociated.

The individual must be reoriented back into the present in order to introduce a **break state**.

The screen should be cleared, either by the subject blanking it out or by the subject opening their eyes, and the process repeated several times*.

To test how effective the change has been, the subject might then try picturing the first cue image. If the swish has worked, the subject will have difficulty doing this.

If the swish has not worked it could be because it was performed too slowly, or the subject failed to blank the screen or open their eyes after each swish. If repeated efforts still fail, then the subject should try producing a more appropriate, less narrowly specified image, or a more desirable and realistic outcome. Or it may be that using size and brightness might not be the appropriate **submodalities** for this subject, in which case they might try substituting two other visual

submodalities, such as colour and distance.
*Bandler suggested five.

SWITCHING
Matching one sensory system by another. An example of *indirect mirroring*. For example pacing an individual's speech tempo (auditory) by nodding one's head at a similar tempo (visual).
[See also *Cross-over Mirroring*]

SYMMETRICAL RELATIONSHIPS
Refers to those relationships in which the more A performs a behaviour, the more B will perform the same or a similar behaviour. For example, if A becomes aggressive then B will become aggressive in response. If B then begins to become calm, A will become calmer in response.
  For example:
A. "Don't you shout at me in that tone of voice!"
B. "Me, shout at you, huh, I'll shout at you any way I want!"
[See *Complementary Relationships*]

SYMPTOMS
Typically the most noticeable, or complained of conscious aspects of the problem or present state. The presenting problem. The *surface structure* representing the *deep structure* of the problem

SYNESTHESIA
A spontaneous link between two or more senses, often used to access an unconscious *representational system*. For example, talking of muted strains, or cold colours. Indeed, colours are frequently used as synesthesias, as in a blue funk, or green with jealousy.
[See also *Overlap*]

SYNONYMY
Sentences of distinct form which have the same meaning,

and the experience which people have with them. In the transformational model of language, two or more sentences derived from the same ***deep structure*** are said to be synonymous. Examples of sentence synonymy are: *The dog licked the bone* and *The bone was licked by the dog*; or *I never trust anybody* and *Nobody is ever trusted by me*.
[See *Transformational Grammar*]

SYNTACTIC AMBIGUITY
Uncertainty as to whether a word ending in "ing" is an adjective or a verb. For example: He has a preference for engaging people in the company.

"HE IS RESPONSIBLE FOR ENGAGING PEOPLE IN THE COMPANY."

SYNTAX
In grammar it refers to the arrangement of words and their relationship with the structure of sentences. In NLP its more usual meaning is the connection within a system of the systematic arrangement of its parts, and the sequence in which internal and external events can be assembled.

SYNTONY
The condition of being syntonic which, in wireless telegraphy, denoted the tuning of transmitting and receiving instruments to a point of congruity. In NLP it signifies being in harmony with oneself and with others. It is the linguistic root of the NLP model Syntonics which is concerned with the process of analysing and producing excellence in communication.

SYSTEM
[See *System Theory*]

SYSTEM THEORY
Short for General System Theory, the idea that the universe is comprised of a hierarchy of seemingly autonomous units. These interrelate with larger units which provide the *context* in which they can survive; whilst in turn providing a context for smaller units contained within themselves. These smaller units are called sub-systems, or holons[20]. A human being therefore may be considered to be a subsystem of the family (see *Family Therapy*); whilst the lymphatic system may be considered as a subsystem of a mammal, or human being.

General System Theory is attributed to Ludvic von Bertalanffy[21]. Ideally, it should be possible to deduce the principles applying to a particular system from the more general theory. In practice this may be problematic.
[See also *Cybernetics, Human Activity System, Natural System*]

THERAPEUTIC METAPHOR
Milton Erickson was an expert at creating metaphors for healing. The following pattern was devised by David Gordon[22].
1. Determine the *context* and individual components {ie the actors, the *context markers*, the behaviours, and beliefs} of the problem situation.
2. Think of an unrelated context may be adopted as the backdrop for a story. This may be fictional, or a real

experience or event.

3. Create (or peg) a series of objects or characters for the story which may be used to represent the individual components of the problem context.

4. Script a story in which the actors in the story encounter a challenge which is analogous to the problem situation. Ensure that each character models the *representational systems*, speech patterns and *meta programmes* of the actors in the original problem.

5. Within the story, suggest the ways in which the story's actors change their *strategies* and overcome the problem.

At no time should the problem be referred to directly whilst the story is being told.

THIRD POSITION
The third of a number of *perceptual positions*. The position of total detachment, giving an objective viewpoint.
[See *Triple Description, Turtles*]

THROUGH TIME
To be *dissociated*. The ability to look at oneself performing a real or imaginary action in either the past, present or future. In other words to be able to step off the *timeline* and to review events past, or future in a sequential way.
[See also: *Dissociation*]

TIMELINE
How our visual, auditory and kinaesthetic states of past, present and future are organised. Two types of timeline have been depicted as "through-time" and "in-time". Someone in through-time will tend to see past, present and future from side to side, is typically well-ordered and has disassociated memories. Someone in in-time will tend to see past, present and future from back to front, tends to live in the present, and may have a less well-ordered time frame, with easy access to associated memories.

Both positions are useful. However, some orientations to

the timeline have limited usefulness. For example walking backwards on the timeline toward the future limits the future to expectations of the past, and has limited desirability.

TONAL
When used to denote a personality type has the same meaning as *Distracter*. However, it has a different meaning within *New Code NLP* where it means anything which has been objectified, or conceptualised via language[7].

TOTE
An acronym standing for **T**est, **O**perate, **T**est, **E**xit. At any one time conscious experience will usually provide a specific signal in one of the five senses: Visual, Auditory, Kinaesthetic, Olfactory or Gustatory. Individuals create *strategies* however by switching between the senses and also between internal and external experience.

TOTEs found their origin in the behaviourist theory of the stimulus-response concept, but the NLP concept is regarded by its originators as a considerable advance on its predecessor as a "neurological model of the formal internal processing sequence triggered by a stimulus".[24] It is also regarded as being a more elegant analysis than other models.

A TOTE comprises the minimum components for any strategy. Stimulus is first received into awareness (or tested). A response is then made, usually via a different sense *(representational system)*. Information is then received ascertaining if the response has had the desired effect (a further test). If all is satisfactory then the strategy ends (the exit).

A simple example of a TOTE is the custom of bowing when being introduced in Japan, or of shaking hands in the West. The TOTE is the basic unit used to identify a particular sequence of behaviour; a strategy is the basic unit of analysis of a particular TOTE or set of TOTEs.

The spelling strategy taught by NLP practitioners is based upon visual recall and kinaesthetic feelings. These form the essential Operate "O" and 2nd Test "T" part of the TOTE.

When an individual reads (V^e) or hears (A^{de}) a word, they commence the strategy "T". They then compare the written word (V^e), (or a visual representation (V^c) they have created as a result hearing the word (A^{de}), with a remembered image of the word (V^r). When these two are the same they feel comfortable (K^i), this confirms for them that the word is correctly spelt "T" and they exit the strategy "E". In cases where the spelling (V^e) does not agree with (V^r) a different feeling will be generated at the second "T" and the individual will loop back to the beginning of the strategy and make the necessary corrections either to their (V^r) or the writing on the paper.

Once installed strategies tend to operate out of conscious awareness as a series of reflexes. Within the spelling strategy, an individual would probably be unaware of making comparisons unless prompted by the kinaesthetic prompt K^i.
[See also *Four Tuple, Relational Operator*]

TOTE NOTATION
A formal way of recording interpersonal, (between individuals and their environment) and intrapersonal (within themselves) communication.

TOTE notation is helpful when modelling the skills of creative individuals, as it enables their strategies to be recorded in a more direct way than by writing in longhand. It stands in relation to NLP as mathematics stands in relation to Philosophy.
[See *Relational Operator, Strategy, TOTE*]

TRANCE
A state wherein the conscious mind is circumvented so as to access resources in the unconscious mind.
[See *Downtime*]

TRANSDERIVATIONAL SEARCH
Accessing the meaning of words by recognising what sights,

sounds or feelings they represent for us, given that words are nothing more than arbitrary labels for the concepts they symbolise.
[See *Language, Semantics*]

TRANSFORMATIONAL GRAMMAR
The relationship between written or spoken language - known as the *surface structure* - and the deeper internal representation from which it springs - known as the *deep structure*. In transformational grammar, or the transformational model of language, a series of rules are provided whereby deep structure is transformed into surface structure in order that we may have clear and comprehensible communication.

This linguistic method of analysis was first suggested by Zellig S. Harris and developed by his pupil *Noam Chomsky*

The English language offers two levels of structure: deep structure and surface structure. Within the deep structure the content, *context*, and relationships may be adduced completely. However, the surface structure, the means by which the sentence is presented to the world lacks such detail. A deep structure is never presented completely in common language instead we have to deduce it using the experience of our culture and *personal history*.

TRANSFORMING [See *Reframing*]

TRIPLE DESCRIPTION
We can perceive our experience in a minimum of three ways according to *John Grinder* and *Judith DeLozier*[23]: the first, second, and third perceptual positions. The first position sees the world from one's own vantage point, without regard for the viewpoint of anyone else. The second position is one in which we can look at the world from another person's point of view. The third position is one of total detachment, giving an objective viewpoint.

However, the third position may not be without affect.

Rather, feelings of comfort may be introduced into third position either by accessing a **core state**, or through the process of **anchoring**. In practice the more 'comfort' that may be introduced into third position, the more 'objective' it may be possible to be about the other positions of a lower logical level.
[See also *Perceptual Position, Turtles, Logical Levels*]

TRUST
An essential ingredient within the context of effective communication, without which one lacks belief in one's power of interaction.
[See *Rapport*]

TUPLE
[See *Four Tuple*]

TURTLES
A well known scientist (Stephen Hawking suggests this was Bertrand Russell, but John Grinder asserts that it was William James; it is conceivably apocryphal) was lecturing on the nature of the Universe. He explained how the earth orbits the sun, and how the sun in turn orbits around the centre of a vast collection of stars known as the galaxy.

After the lecture a small, slightly built lady of mature years approached him saying. "It was a very interesting lecture, young man; but in fact the world is supported on the back of a large tortoise".

The scientist smiled, gently and politely asked the old lady: "If that is so madam, then what does the tortoise stand upon".

She laughed as if he was an impish boy and retorted: "You don't catch me out like that young man, it's turtles all the way down".
[See: *Grinder, John, Logical Levels, Metaphor, New Code NLP, Perceptual Position*]

UNCONSCIOUS
That which is not in present moment awareness.

UNIFIED FIELD
The unified field which owes its existence to **Robert Dilts**, It is a three-dimensional model for dealing with personal change, based on neurological levels, perceptual position, and time.

The deepest level is the spiritual level; the external level is the environment; to reach the environmental level from the spiritual level, we pass through the levels of identity, belief, capability, and behaviour.

The spiritual level is the core of our beliefs and actions. Identity is the basic sense of our self and our values. Beliefs comprise those ideas, both permissive and limiting, on which we base our actions. Capability comprises our behaviour, skills, and strategies. Behaviour are those actions we perform despite our capability. Environment consists of our surroundings and people with whom we come in contact.

The key to the unified field is balance: individuals may become unbalanced by placing too much importance on the element of time, e.g. by too much concern over past events. They may spend too much time in one of three or more [see *Triple Description*]. Or there may be a lack of balance in one of the neurological levels. [See *Turtles*]

UNIVERSAL QUANTIFIERS
Generalisations which do not admit of any exceptions to an individual's statement, such as "every", "never", and "all". The *meta model* response in order expand the individual's learned limitation might be: "Can you think of a time when. . .?" or "Can you think of anyone who. . .?" in order to force the individual into awareness of contradictions to the statement. Alternatively the statement could be repeated, in an exaggerated manner, to demonstrate its implausibility or absurdity.

UNSPECIFIED NOUNS

Nouns that are non-specific about the "who" and "what" of an activity. A noun often has more than one dictionary definition; nouns, furthermore, are capable of meaning different things to different people, or different things in different circumstances. Questioning "Who, or what, specifically?" is the appropriate way to establish and to clarify an unspecified noun.

Statement: "Some of our staff have serious complaints." Questions: "Who specifically? What complaints specifically?"
[See *Meta-Model*]

UNSPECIFIED VERBS

Verbs that delete such details of an activity as when, where, or how it occurred, how long it lasted, and how stimulating it was. *meta model* questions such as "Where specifically?", "Specifically when?", and "How specifically?"; will restore a meaningful context into the statements.

For example: "I'll do that when I've got more time." Question: "How, specifically, will you do it?"

UPTIME
A mental state where our senses are tuned to the outside world and our attention is focused outwards. [See *Downtime*]

VALUES
Those (mainly unconscious) beliefs that we acquire from external "parental-type" influences, or subsequently by choice, and which motivate us and the direction we take in life. Specific values, in NLP, are described as ***criteria*** and are frequently ***nominalizations*** .

V
A symbol representing *Visual* in ***TOTE notation***.

V^c
A symbol representing Visual Constructed.

VISUAL
Pertaining to the sense of sight. When used to describe a person, it has the same meaning as ***blamer***.

V^r
A symbol representing Visual Remembered.

VISUAL SCRAMBLE
A form of two-handed ***link***. When using the hands as links, a visual scramble is achieved by bringing the hands together and clasping them at an appropriate moment. This enables the subject to integrate two sets of information (represented symbolically by each of the hands) on an unconscious level.

This is sometimes called a visual squash.
[See *Anchoring*]

VISUALISATION
The process of creating a mental image. The use of the visual system to experience internal or external data.
[See *Eye Accessing Cues, Representational Systems*]

VITAL SIGNS
Observable or implied patterns which have been coded into the structure of NLP [See *Score Model*]. For example: *accessing cues*, *predicate patterns*, *meta model* patterns, posture and gesture, *submodalities*, *meta programme* patterns, *criteria*, *values* and *beliefs*.

VOICE MATCHING
A means of achieving *rapport* by matching the tone, tempo, volume and rhythm of one's speech to that of another person.
[See *Matching, Pacing*]

WELL-FORMED
Meeting some set of conditions about form. Well-formed in language would thus consist in the language being semantically and syntactically valid. Within NLP well-formedness refers to having *outcomes* which conform to specific rules which increase the possibility of achievement.

WELL-FORMEDNESS CRITERIA
Those criteria used in choosing an *outcome* which is well formed in the sense that it is expressed in a positive way (i.e. what I want, not what I do not want), is specific, is reasonably achievable, is not too large (in which event it will need to be broken down into smaller chunks) and does not offend ecological considerations.
[See *Chunking*]

REFERENCES

(1) Usage and Abusage, Eric Partridge, Hamish Hamilton, 1947

(2) Frogs Into Princes, Richard Bandler and John Grinder, Real People Press, 1979

(3) Using Your Brain For a Change, Richard Bandler, Real People Press, 1985

(4) Steps to an Ecology of Mind, Gregory Bateson, Ballantine Books, 1972

(5) Helping Families to Change, Virginia Satir, High Hills Comprehensive Community Mental Health Center, 1972

(6) Core Transformation, Reaching the Wellspring Within, Connirae Andreas with Tamara Andreas, Moab, 1994

(7) The Structure of Magic, Volume 1, Richard Bandler and John Grinder, Science and Behaviour Books, 1975

(8) Peoplemaking, Virginia Satir, Science and Behaviour Books, 1972

(9) The Fire From Within, Carlos Castaneda, Simon & Schuster, 1984

(10) Living Awareness: A Heart-warming Approach to NLP, Peter Wrycza, Gateway Books, 1977

(11) The Tyranny of Words, Stuart Chase, Methuen, 1938

(12) The Basis of Personality, James Tad, Profitability Consulting, 1987

(13) The Magical Number Seven, Plus or Minus Two, George Miller, Psychology Review Volume 83, 1957

(14) The Structure of the Brain, Miller, Galanter and Pribram, Henry Holt & Co., 1960

(15) Language in Thought and Actiion, S.I. Hayakawa, Harcourt, Brace & World, 1963

(16) Magic in Action, Richard Bandler, Meta Publications, 1992

(17) The Meaning of Meaning, C.K. Ogden and L.A. Richards, Kegan Paul, 1944

(18) The Spirit of NLP, Michael L. Head, Anglo American Books, 1996

(19) The Psychobiology of Mind Body Healing, Ernest L. Rossi, Norton, 1986

(20) Janus, Arthur Koestler, Hutchinson, 1978

(21) General System Theory, Ludwig von Bertalanffy, Brunner, 1968

(22) Therapeutic Metaphors, David Gordon, Meta Publications, 1978

(23) Turtles All the Way Down, Judith DeLozier and John Grinder, DeLozier and Associates, 1987

(24) Neuro-Linguistic Programming, Vol. 1, Robert Dilts, John Grinder, Richard Bandler and Judith DeLozier, Meta Publications, 1980.